Contents

Introduction — 3

1 Planning

1.1 Employment contexts — 4
Funding policies
Flexible working
New legislation

1.2 Employment principles — 6
Legal obligations
Codes of practice

1.3 Personal responsibilities — 8
Take responsibility for your new role
Clarify your worker's role and responsibilities
Procedures for the employment relationship
Be willing to learn from secular sources

1.4 Employment resources — 9
Public bodies
Voluntary sector sources
Trade union sources

2 Appointing

2.1 Setting up the basic structures — 11
Checking legal structures
Forming a working group
Setting a timetable

2.2 Defining what you need — 12
Writing the job description
Person specification
Designing an application form
Advertising

2.3 Selecting what you need — 16
Shortlisting
Before the interview
During the interview

2.4 Securing your worker — 18
Making a job offer
Checks and references
Drawing up a contract of employment

The Project Worker, a guide to employing staff in church projects
© The Church Urban Fund, 2000

3	Working	
3.1	Financial responsibilities Pay Income tax and National Insurance Pensions Statutory Sick Pay/Statutory Maternity Pay	21
3.2	Health and safety Employer's responsibilities Management of health and safety Health and safety policies Insurance	23
3.3	Disciplinary and grievance procedures Disciplinary procedure Grievance procedure	25
3.4	Monitoring and assessment Probationary periods Reviews Supervision	28
3.5	Support and development Induction programmes Support Training	30

4	Reviewing	
4.1	Evaluating the work	33
4.2	Concluding the work Selection Consultation Notice periods Redundancy payments Paid time off Support References Policy	34
4.3	Continuing the work Fundraising Contract renewal	37
4.4	Redeveloping the work	38

Appendix A: Useful resources	40
Appendix B: Useful addresses	42

Introduction

If you have decided to read this guide, it is likely that congratulations are in order. Your vision for your project has succeeded in convincing a funding body of the value of your work. Given the strength of the competition for grants to support local work, this is an achievement of which you may be proud.

The proof of your success is that you now have the money you need to employ the worker (or even workers) you need to make your vision a reality. No doubt you are keen to have someone in post as quickly as possible. However, in becoming an employer, you are assuming major responsibilities in an area of which you may have either no, or very limited, experience. Moreover, given that legislation governing the recruitment and employment of staff is constantly changing, any experience you may have had in the past is likely to be outdated. It is important to take your responsibilities seriously and to prepare carefully for your new role as the employer of a paid worker.

If you find this prospect overwhelming, *The Project Worker* is intended to address your need. It has been written specifically (but not exclusively) for individuals and groups responsible for church-related projects who are about to undertake responsibility for the appointment and management of paid staff. It is assumed, in the first instance, that your success in fundraising means that your project is constituted in such a way that enables you to employ a worker. It is also assumed that the relationship you seek is with an employee (as opposed to a freelance or agency worker) and that—in the vast majority of cases—the contract is likely to be offered on a fixed-term basis.

The four main sections of the guide will help you to think through the implications of your new role and responsibilities and to manage the practicalities of the employment relationship from the initial planning stage through to its conclusion:

- **Planning** invites you to consider the wider employment context so that you can develop an appropriate and responsible practice

- **Appointing** sets out the steps involved in selecting and appointing your worker so that you can manage the process fairly and professionally

- **Working** summarises issues relating to management and support once your new worker is in post that will enable the work of the project to progress smoothly

- **Reviewing** considers the options available at the end of the period of funding to enable decisions and future planning for project and worker

It may be tempting to concentrate on the section that meets your immediate need and to leave the others for future reference. Although help with the selection and appointment process is the main emphasis of the guide, you are strongly recommended to work through all four sections so that potential problems and pitfalls further down the line can be anticipated and avoided in the planning stage.

Above all, the guide encourages you to realise a single, long-term objective: the development of structures and practices that will enable the new project worker to carry the vision for your project forward.

To help you further, a bibliography and list of contacts point you in the direction of any additional resources you may need. *The Project Worker* is essentially an introduction to the issues: as an employer you are likely to come up against particular situations in which more detailed information will be required. It should also be emphasised that, although effort has been made to ensure that information is accurate and up-to-date, the content is not intended to be legally comprehensive.

Acknowledgements

We are grateful for the contributions of various people. Joy Madieros (Southern Secretary and Human Resources Director, YMCA England) drew attention to the importance of incoming pensions legislation; Julian Holywell (Parish Resources Officer, Manchester Diocesan Board for Church & Society) contributed ideas on project sustainability and offered practical strategies for accessing new sources of funds. We would also like to thank those management committee members and workers whose positive and negative experiences of employment in small, church-based community projects enliven the pages of the guide.

1 Planning

In becoming an employer you should have two main priorities: to take your new responsibilities seriously and to give careful attention to the establishment of structures that will enable and support both worker and project.

This section focuses on the preparatory thinking which will help you to do that. It provides an overview of three trends which affect employment in Britain today and gives the opportunity to consider the implications of each trend for your own practice. You are also invited to consider basic principles appropriate to the current employment context which might inform your practice. Finally, you are directed towards the resources that assist the employment process.
A checklist of issues to address in your planning is appended.

1.1 Employment contexts

Employment in Britain has changed dramatically in the last two decades and it is helpful to begin with an overview of three major trends: short-termism in funding; the rise of flexible working practices; and the development of employment legislation to meet new needs. As you will discover, each of these has practical implications for organisations in the voluntary sector, which is the sector of the economy within which most church-related community projects are located.

Funding policies

Your search for project funding will have brought you face to face with one of the most important factors affecting employment: money for projects, except in a few rare and fortunate cases, is usually only awarded for a fixed period.

This has implications for private and public sector employers, where contracts of employment may be shaped by the duration of a successful funding bid. The impact on voluntary sector organisations is especially serious, because they rely heavily on grants to support workers. These are not only becoming harder to access, but also increasingly short-term. One experienced project manager considers that, 'any expansion of our work will be for projects which will be two or three years long... in our terms, that's long-term.' Moreover, since such grants are seen as 'pump-priming' for projects, there is often no, or very limited, opportunity for them to be renewed.

Some projects are more likely to experience the negative impact of current funding policies than others. A project offering a core service, such as a nursery, meets a need that is almost certain to outlast the end of a funding period. It is likely to struggle more than a project with a specific, time-limited goal, such as the organisation of a community group to influence plans for redeveloping the area, which may be met within the funding period.

Despite the considerable challenge of securing continuation funding, core service projects that set targets, demonstrate that they have been met and redevelop to meet new needs will find that their chances are greatly improved.

It is therefore essential to be clear about the nature of your project (core service or fixed-term) from the outset and to have some ideas about its future beyond the end of the funding period. There are different options: improved development of the same service; the development of a new project (which may build on the work of the first); or even closure following achievement of goals.

Whatever the nature of your project and plans for its future, you also need to remember that your funder is primarily interested in the development of the work (not the worker).

Funding policies have major implications for your employment practice: any post created as a result of a successful funding bid is likely to be fixed-term (and possibly part-time), rather than full-time and permanent. In fact, to offer a permanent or open contract when funding is only for a limited period is a recipe for complications when the money runs out. These may affect your legal and personal relationship with the worker and, in a worst case scenario, may also damage the viability of the project itself.

Although this may seem strange, it is best to acknowledge the 'life expectancy' of the employment relationship from the outset. This will help design and manage the post appropriately for the duration of your current funding and prioritise the development of fundraising strategies should you wish to retain paid workers once your period of funding has ended. You will find more information on the available options in Section 4.

Flexible working

Hesitation about full-time permanent contracts is not just an issue for small projects dependent upon short-term funding: labour market flexibility has been a key issue for employers and workers throughout the last 20 years. The 'job for life', we are told, is fast disappearing, if not already dead. In its place comes the new 'flexible working', a catch-all term which has at least six different dimensions. The two which are likely to be most relevant to your practice are numerical flexibility, which allows the employer to vary staff numbers (for example, through fixed-term, temporary and casual posts) and temporal flexibility, which allows employers to vary working hours (for example, via part-time working, job-sharing, flexi-time and reduced hours). Note that temporal and numerical flexibility often overlap: it is possible to work part-time on a fixed-term contract. If you look at the appointments section of any newspaper, you will find that such contracts are not unusual.

The demise of the full-time, permanent post is probably over-exaggerated. However, the voluntary sector is believed to employ a higher proportion of flexible workers than the private or public sectors. A 1996 survey by the Manufacturing Science and Finance Union (MSF) found that 20 per cent of organisations employed casual or sessional workers and that 42 per cent employed workers on fixed-term contracts. Evidence from the umbrella body, the National Council for Voluntary Organisation (NCVO), also suggests that the voluntary sector makes greater than average use of part-time workers. This partly reflects the funding constraints already described. In addition, many charities and community projects find that the full-time, nine to five model is inappropriate to the service they offer.

You will need to consider the options for your project: what working arrangements will best suit the constraints of your project's budget and the nature of your work? Guidance on how to define your needs more clearly is included in Section 2.

Flexibility is double-edged. On the plus side, it can give a project more freedom to develop creative responses to local needs. One project manager observes that, 'it makes you think carefully what the job is and what the output or outcomes are.' Meanwhile, flexible working may enable project workers to achieve a better balance between home and working life. A community worker comments, 'I find that if I'm working in an area for too long, I lose the distance needed to do the job properly.'

On the other hand, flexibility has a downside. As the project manager puts it, 'people are a bit cavalier—here today, gone tomorrow—nobody has any hold on each other.' Moreover, from the employee's perspective, fixed-term and part-time contracts, even if their use is not deliberately exploitative, can create insecurity.

If the full-time, permanent model of employment is not appropriate to the needs of your project, you will need to ensure that flexibility in the employment relationship disadvantages neither the worker nor the work.

New legislation

Until relatively recently, the balance of flexibility was in favour of the employer as workers' rights were steadily eroded. However, in the late 1990s, the bias against the employee was steadily redressed. New employment legislation, much of which originates from European directives on equal opportunities and health and safety, is now in force in the United Kingdom. This seeks to close the loopholes which left workers employed on flexible contracts vulnerable to exploitation by their employers. Part-time and fixed-term workers in particular now enjoy much better legal protection than they did in the 1980s and early 1990s. Recent decisions at the European level suggest that the position of workers employed on fixed-term contracts is soon to be strengthened still further.

Whether you welcome or regret the strengthening of workers' rights in new legislation, you cannot ignore the consequences for your own practice. Even small, first-time employers are affected.

Box A summarises the most important examples of new and incoming legislation which will affect your role as employer. Note that the first two items, on working time and the minimum wage, are already in force. In both areas you are now bound to observe minimum standards. The third item, which affects issues such as parental leave and pensions, has just reached the statute books (although not every provision comes into force immediately). The fourth, on pensions, is in the pipeline. You are not yet bound by its proposals, but it is important to be aware of their implications for your own employment practice. Projects making appointments on a fixed-term or part-time basis must also remember that new employment legislation increasingly applies to all workers, and not just to permanent, full-time employees.

Failure to comply with your new responsibilities will have serious legal consequences, and other issues—such as pensions—have implications for your future budgets. However, the argument in favour of legislation is as much based on the carrot as it is on the stick. Incoming proposals, such as those contained in the Employment Relations Bill (1999), can make a positive difference to practice. In the words of Paul Boateng, the minister responsible for the voluntary sector, 'if we want a healthy and growing voluntary sector, it is important that workers don't feel ripped off, don't feel taken advantage of.' More importantly, from the perspective of the individual project, willingness to fulfil your responsibilities is likely to improve your relationship with your worker.

Box A: New and incoming employment legislation

Working Time Regulations came into effect in October 1998. They provide a limit of 48 hours on the working week; the right to a break of at least 20 minutes in six hours' work; and the right to three weeks paid holiday (increased to four weeks in 1999). Some groups of workers are exempt, but in general the regulations are statutory minimum rights which apply to all workers (including trainees, agency workers and part-time workers). They cannot be used to reduce better rights acquired via a contract of employment or through custom and practice in the workplace. Employers are responsible for making sure that their contracts and working practices comply with the regulations. If workers are refused their statutory rights or victimised for claiming them, they may take their case to an Employment Tribunal.

The National Minimum Wage came into effect on 1 April 1999. Most workers in the country (including those who are not counted as employees) are now entitled by law to a minimum hourly rate of pay. The main rate is £3.60 per hour, but workers aged 18 to 21 and those who are in the first six months of working for a new employer and undergoing accredited training, currently receive a lower hourly rate. (New legislation does not, however, diminish contractual rights to better terms.) In addition to ensuring minimum rates of pay, employers are responsible for keeping records to show how they have been calculated. These must be kept for a minimum of three years, although—given that the period in which workers can bring breach of contract claims before a civil court for underpayment is six years—a longer period is recommended. Without records an employer would have difficulty in defending claims either in court or before minimum wage inspectors.

The Employment Relations Bill, popularly known as 'fairness at work', came into force in July 1999. It covers a wide range of issues, which can be divided into three main groups: procedures for union recognition; the right of trade unions to accompany any worker to a disciplinary or grievance procedure (regardless of whether or not they are union members); and parental leave. The last group includes proposals to extend the period of paid maternity leave; to entitle all parents (including adoptive parents) to three months of leave; and the right to unpaid time off to deal with an urgent domestic incident. In addition there are new rights for part-time workers; protection from dismissal in some cases of industrial action; and protection against employer blacklists of union activists.

Partnership in Pensions is a paper setting out proposals for pension reform. It will be some years before the new system delivers in full, but new 'stakeholder pensions' (a public/private partnership) are likely to have serious administrative and financial implications for employers. The voluntary sector, where fewer than 15 per cent of employers (and only four per cent of organisations in the £10,000 to £100,000 income bracket) offer some form of pension scheme to their workers, will be particularly affected. In order to avoid being overtaken by legislation, it is increasingly important to include pensions in staff budgets.

1.2 Employment principles

Given a shifting, complex context, what principles should inform your employment practice? Three categories, each with a different legal status, are set out below: legal obligations; codes of good practice; and personal responsibilities.

Legal obligations

The first duty of an employer, reinforced by the new emphasis on employment legislation, is to be aware of legal responsibilities. Box B summarises the statutory rights (those set out in law) currently afforded to all employees: in the majority of cases, these now apply to part-time, fixed-term, temporary and casual workers as well as to full-time, permanent employees.

In addition to their statutory rights, employees have contractual rights (those given as part of the contract of employment).

Box B: Employee's statutory rights

From the first day of employment, employees have the right:
- to the National Minimum Wage
- to paid leave and rest set out under the Working Time Directive
- to equal pay for work of equal value
- not to be discriminated against on grounds of race
- not to be discriminated against on grounds of sex or marital status
- not to be discriminated on grounds of disability (in organisations with 15 or more workers)
- to work in a safe, healthy environment
- to union membership and participation in union activities
- to protection against victimisation or dismissal on grounds of union membership, union activities, complaints about health and safety, or the assertion of statutory rights
- to reasonable time off with pay to perform duties as a recognised trade union official or employee representative, or as a safety representative (in organisations of more than five staff)
- to reasonable time off (which need not be paid) for participation in the activities of a recognised trade union, or public activities
- to statutory sick pay
- to compensation in the event of illness or injury arising from the course of employment
- not to disclose, or be penalised for a failure to disclose, spent convictions (except in certain circumstances such as work with children)

In addition, female employees have a statutory entitlement to:
- paid time off for ante-natal care
- 18 weeks' maternity leave
- return to the same job on the same pay and conditions after 18 weeks' maternity leave
- not to be dismissed for any reason connected with their pregnancy

Continuous service with an employer gives employees the right:
- to a statement of employment particulars within two months of starting work (one calendar month qualifying period)
- not to be unfairly dismissed (one year qualifying period)
- to longer maternity leave (some of it paid) and the right to return to work at the end of this leave (one year qualifying period)

Codes of practice

What else can employers committed to the principle of good practice do, in addition to fulfilling their legal obligations towards employees? Some may wish to 'go the second mile' by signing up to voluntary codes of practice: the Equal Opportunities Commission and the Commission for Racial Equality produce examples, listed in Appendix A.

Codes of practices can be used to support and improve practice both for employees and for all project users and workers. The development of an equal opportunities statement (a declaration of your opposition to discrimination and plans for eliminating it) and equal opportunities policy (a more detailed plan of action) for your project is strongly recommended, if you do not already have these in place. You may use them as an opportunity to extend your commitment to equal opportunities beyond the legal minimum—for example, by improving access for workers with disabilities—or to groups currently without legal protection—for example, gay men and lesbians or older workers.

A word of caution. Projects should be wary of committing themselves to procedures that cannot be sustained. A code may have been developed for larger organisations in a different economic climate. It may not be appropriate to a small, struggling project and specific provisions may actually be unworkable. For example, a project committed to equal opportunities may wish to advertise all posts in every community language: but, unless the project has the budget to support this, the commitment cannot be realised.

A project manager who faced this issue comments, 'some procedures seemed to operate on a level which wasn't related to how you were funded, or the daily realities of running an organisation—that's had to be modified in the light of reality.'

As the Commission for Racial Equality points out in its *Race Relations Code of Practice* in relation to small firms, the requirement is not conformity to every detailed recommendation, but ensuring that 'practices are consistent with the Code's general intentions'.

Without a realistic, responsible approach, codes of practice are likely to remain fine words. It is important, if they are to become a reality, to ensure that your equal opportunities policy develops within the situation in which you are operating. Consequently, the approach adopted in this guide is to handle equal opportunities issues as a practical consideration to be taken into account within the contexts in which they arise, rather than as an abstract ideal.

1.3 Personal responsibilities

Unlike legal obligations and codes of practice, you are unlikely to find this third category of principles in employment literature. The following guidelines are equally important, because they require prospective employers to consider their role and responsibilities on a personal, day-to-day level.

Take responsibility for your new role

The principle may seem obvious, but even well-established projects have been known to fail this responsibility. You need to clarify from the outset who actually employs your worker. Generally speaking, apart from situations where workers are managed by a central structure, workers are employed by the management committee of their project. You have a legal responsibility to name the employing body in the contract of employment (see Section 2). This is important for practical reasons: should a problem arise, the situation is further complicated if no one is prepared to take responsibility. However, taking on the role of employer also has implications for your management of the employment relationship.

If you are a member of the employing body, your relationship with the project worker should be defined by that role. It is to be hoped that personal friendships will spring from the working relationship, but you must always remember that your own role is primarily that of employer rather than advocate, counsellor or friend. This principle applies whether the worker is someone appointed from outside your community, or someone already known to you as a project volunteer, a church member or a local resident. If the worker is drawn from existing networks, it may be even more important to define the change in the nature of your relationship with them. There is no need to be heavy-handed, but if difficulties do arise, it is your responsibility as the employer to have ensured that appropriate boundaries are established.

The importance of this principle cannot be over-emphasised. The priority of the employer cannot always be to promote the interests of the worker. You have a responsibility towards your employees, but also responsibilities towards funding bodies and the future of the project itself. A manager of a church-sponsored employment project concludes, 'You have ethical responsibilities to staff, but you have an ethical responsibility to society to create innovative projects and services which match people's needs.'

Juggling different interests is a complex but essential skill. Sometimes interests conflict and difficult decisions have to be made. By taking responsibility for your role, you prevent confusion between the professional and personal relationships you have with your staff. You will find examples of situations in which boundaries are easily blurred in the discussion of the distinction between supervision and support in Section 3. The issues are probably sharpest in situations when a worker must be made redundant. This is discussed in more depth in Section 4.

Clarify your worker's role and responsibilities

The principle is, in the first instance, about tasks. You have a vision for the project and now the resources to realise your vision through the employment of a paid worker. But what, exactly, will your new project worker actually do?

The way to think this through is by drawing up a job description. You will find more information on how to do this in Section 2. The principle also has implications for relationships within the project. You need to think how the worker's role and responsibilities relate to the differing roles and responsibilities of others involved in the project, such as volunteers or clergy. If you employ more than one worker, you will need to consider how they might best complement each other and how particular responsibilities will be assigned.

In a small project, where the prevailing culture is 'all hands on deck', tasks are shared and roles may blur in practice. It is perfectly acceptable to acknowledge the need for such flexibility in the job description. It is not acceptable to put unfair pressure on workers either to take on responsibilities beyond their job description or to work beyond their contractual hours. A worker employed at a church-based youth project reports, 'I regularly worked well above the hours I was supposed to, but when I raised this with management was made to feel that I shouldn't complain as "the vicar was never off the job".'

One of the most frequently reported characteristics of workers in the voluntary sector is their high degree of commitment. This asset is of immense benefit to your project and should never be exploited.

Procedures for the employment relationship

In small organisations, especially where people know each other and personal relationships are strong, there can be a tendency to neglect formal procedures. Such procedures become very important the moment paid employment is involved.

It is, as you already know, illegal to discriminate on grounds of sex, marital status, race and disability and an equal opportunities procedure in recruitment may be a condition of your funding. Even where this is not the case, if a project has, say, four regular volunteers interested in the new post, you will need to ensure that your selection and appointment process is both open and fair.

In this way you will avoid the problem which arose within a community project supported by trust money, where the community worker discovered that, in contravention of the terms of the funding, 'the manager, a local person, was offering jobs only to people in her personal networks.'

Quite apart from the terms of your grant, it is in the best interests of your project to ensure that procedures are directed towards finding the best person for the job. You will find more information on how to run an equal opportunities appointment process in Section 2.

Procedures are also important whenever grievances and disciplinary issues arise. Experience indicates that a purely personal approach is rarely adequate as a means of resolving workplace disputes. A trade union organiser with many years of experience observes, 'when there's a dispute within a voluntary organisation, it can be as vicious and personal as a family feud.'

It is therefore important, even if you think that you will never have recourse to them, to set up appropriate policies and procedures to deal with disciplinary issues and grievances in advance. These act as a safeguard for all parties, defusing potential problems before they become complicated and costly. If such policies are applied consistently, and are seen to be applied consistently, charges of unfairness will be avoided. An added benefit is that clear procedures may help to prevent disputes from arising in the first place. You will find more information on both these issues in Section 3.

Be willing to learn from secular sources
A church project may naturally look first to its own structures for guidance. In addition to this guide, churches and church organisations have produced resources which may be relevant to your needs. Some dioceses within the Church of England have their own comprehensive guides to 'best practice' on the employment of community workers and the Roman Catholic Church has a collection of loose-leaf papers on the employment of lay people in pastoral work. Meanwhile, the Methodist Church is currently updating a pack on the employment of lay workers and the Baptist Union is preparing a leaflet for local churches.

Such denominational resources are often of high quality, with the additional advantage of being tailored to particular situations. However, despite their quality, they may be produced primarily as 'in-house' publications and not widely publicised beyond the audiences for whom they were originally intended.

It is worth checking whether resources are available within your own structures, or if other guides have been written with church projects in mind. It is also strongly recommended that you look beyond the churches for advice on employment issues. This is because, although the employment of lay workers is increasingly common, the clergy still constitute the major human resources in most churches. But clergy are not employees. Consequently, the relationship between clergy and congregations is not an appropriate model for other employment relationships.

To help you explore other alternatives, this section concludes with an overview of the additional resources available to help church-based projects develop more appropriate models (see also Appendix A).

1.4 Employment resources

If you look further afield, you will have access to a wider range of high quality material. The main sources of information can be divided into three groups: public bodies, voluntary organisations and trade unions. Asterisks indicate that contact information is provided in Appendix B. Basic information from any of these sources is either available free, or priced at a level even a small project on a limited budget can afford.

Public bodies
You cannot, as an employer, avoid contact with the Inland Revenue* and the Inland Revenue Contributions Agency*. The positive aspect of this is access to leaflets and helplines which will inform you of your new responsibilities and advise you on how to proceed. In addition, there are other public bodies which you may not have thought of accessing, but are extremely useful sources of information and guidance. The Advisory, Conciliation and Arbitration Service (ACAS)* produces, among other resources, a series of low-cost leaflets on employment issues for small firms; the Health and Safety Executive (HSE)* provides specialist advice on health and safety policies and insurance; and the Equal Opportunities Commission* and the Commission for Racial Equality* will help you develop a non-discriminatory recruitment process and employment practice.

You may also wish to investigate written or other sources of help provided by your local authority: given that some funding bids have to be channelled through local authorities, they have an interest in ensuring that projects are securely founded and well-managed.

Voluntary sector sources
In addition to general information available from public sources, there is another source specifically tailored to your needs. For, as the numbers working in the voluntary sector rise—NCVO* estimates that the sector now employs more than 500,000 full and part-time workers—and legislation becomes more complex, advice and the dissemination of good practice has become a priority. NCVO produces regular, free briefing papers on employment issues and has recently updated its comprehensive *Good Employment Guide for the Voluntary Sector*. This manual, although rather more expensive than similar guides, is a good investment since purchase also entitles the buyer to access a

helpdesk. First-time or inexperienced employers are also recommended to consult catalogues of the Directory of Social Change*, which advertise practical guides for projects on general and specific topics. You will find a selection of the most useful and affordable publications produced by the Directory of Social Change and other organisations listed in Appendix A.

In addition to general guides for projects, there are others focusing on specific issues. The Pensions Trust* provides pensions for employees in the voluntary sector; New Ways to Work* is a first-rate resource for projects wishing to adopt or find out more about good practice in flexible working arrangements; and the Maternity Alliance* can advise on how to fulfil your responsibilities towards an employee who is expecting to take maternity leave.

Trade union sources

People involved in the daily management of small, church-based projects may not automatically think of trade unions. However, as a prospective employer, you should be aware that unions are becoming more active in the voluntary sector, in which workers (especially in small organisations) can be very isolated and unsupported.

UNISON*, the Transport and General Workers Union (TGWU)* and MSF* are the three main players: MSF has a particular interest in the rights of church workers. It is therefore important for employers to approach this positively and take advantage of the many resources produced by unions on workplace issues. These publications are, of course, written from the employee's perspective. However, their big plus is that they are on top of the very latest developments in employment law, health and safety and equality issues. A key source is the Labour Research Department (LRD)*, which produces a wide range of booklets on the latest issues. The most recent LRD catalogue at time of writing (May 1999) includes both guides to new legislation such as the Minimum Wage and analyses of incoming legislation such as the Employment Relations Bill. Moreover, LRD publications explain the complexities in terms that a non-specialist can easily understand.

Checklist

You now have an overview of context, principles and resources, and it is appropriate to address some of their implications for your own project. The following questions are designed to stimulate 'first thoughts' within your group. You will find more detail on how to ground your ideas in practice in the following sections.

✔ Have you decided who is going to be the employer?

✔ Given your funding, what length of contract is it possible for you to offer?

✔ If the contract is fixed-term, do you have any initial ideas about what might happen when the funding runs out? Is a full-time, nine to five contract appropriate to the needs of your project?

✔ If not, what other possibilities are open to you? And what are their implications for the worker? And for the project? And funding?

✔ What resources do you need to consult? What others are available locally? Who is to be responsible for checking them out?

2 Appointing

Having considered the context in which you seek to employ a worker, outlined the principles you aim to apply, and reviewed available resources, you are ready to begin the recruitment process. This section takes you through four stages: setting up basic structures; identifying the key tasks of the job and skills required; making your selection; and securing the appointment.

You must take equal opportunities issues into account throughout. In keeping with the approach of this guide, these are considered as they arise. For more detail on the implementation of equal opportunities in recruitment, consult the Equal Opportunities Commission* and the Commission for Racial Equality*.

Remember, too, that your recruitment must take account of legislation to protect the rights of disabled workers and former offenders, and ensure that your worker has permission to live and work in the UK.

2.1 Setting up the basic structures

Before you begin the paperwork, satisfy yourself that the legal structure of your project is appropriate to your new responsibilities; set up a working group with responsibility for the appointment process; and prepare a flexible timetable to work to.

Checking legal structures

This guide assumes your project is so constituted that you are able to employ a worker. This means that detailed analyses of the full range of legal structures are not included. It is worth noting that the two structures commonly chosen by community projects have very different implications for their liabilities as an employer.

Many voluntary organisations are unincorporated associations—individuals who agree to work together for a common purpose. Unencumbered by heavy organisational structures, a project organised on this basis may design and implement its own rules, provided no laws are broken. But in the event of legal action associated with the employment or activities of a worker, members of the management committee may become personally liable. This applies to recruitment: when an Employment Tribunal upheld complaints of sexual discrimination by two unsuccessful applicants for a senior post, members of the management committee of a regional Race Equality Council were left with a hefty bill. The organisation closed—nine jobs were lost.

An employment lawyer considers that the case, 'shows the danger of voluntary organisations taking staff on and incurring considerable liability without the protection of company status.'

Projects, especially if they plan to employ more staff, are advised to 'incorporate' to gain limited liability status. If a local church is the employer incorporation may be unnecessary. If this does not apply to your project, the usual route is to form a company limited by guarantee. This means a project must comply with company and charity law and is obliged to file accounts and other documents at the required time.

If company status is not appropriate to your project, you may wish to consider forming a trust, registering as an industrial or provident society, or as a cooperative or community cooperative. Fuller information on the implications of different legal structures is found in publications in Appendix A: the manual produced by the Diocese of Birmingham Board for Social Responsibility is especially helpful on the legal basis of church projects.

You may still consider that unincorporated status is most appropriate for your project. If so, to protect the interests of the project and the management committee, all your employment procedures must be meticulously drawn up and implemented.

Forming a working group

If you are satisfied with your project's legal structure, the next task is to form your working group. It is likely that, in the initial stages of designing the job description and person specification, the work will be undertaken and/or agreed by the whole management committee.

This may prove time-consuming. The advantage is that the tasks to be undertaken by the worker, and the criteria for selection, are agreed by all who will carry responsibility for the worker. This avoids disagreement during the selection process, which is not only embarrassing and unprofessional, but could lose the project a strong candidate. A youth worker describes an interview in which members of the panel 'kept arguing whether the post was about evangelism or not—it was obvious that there were different agendas.' Not surprisingly, she refused the job. The absence of agreement on the aims of the post was a strong indicator to expect, at best, only partial support from her management committee, and, at worst, an impossible working brief.

It may be best for your project to involve others in the appointment process: specialists in your denomination may advise on terms and conditions; other local churches or ecumenical bodies may offer support (for example, by advertising the post); and representatives of other community organisations or the local authority working in a similar area may have valuable expertise which you might use on your interviewing panel.

Whatever the composition of your group, ensure that the same people are involved throughout. Once you have achieved consensus on the main elements of the post and the skills required, specific tasks may be usefully delegated.

Setting a timetable

The process of appointment may take longer than you think. Thirteen weeks is the probable minimum from writing a job description to the worker's starting date.

Think of the timescale as three stages: defining what you need (job description, person specification, advertisement, application form); selecting what you need (shortlisting and interviews); securing your worker (checks and references, a formal job offer and contract of employment). The first two stages are within your control, but allow a degree of flexibility in the third. The timescale assumes that you make an appointment; that your preferred candidate accepts; and that only four weeks' notice will be required.

2.2 Defining what you need

This phase involves working through a series of tasks: writing the job description; preparing a person specification; compiling an application form/pack; and writing your advertisement. It is important that tasks are tackled in this order, so that your recruitment process is not driven by an image of the kind of person who will 'fit in'. Focusing on the requirements of the job ensures equal opportunities for applicants, so providing you with a wider range from which to select.

Writing the job description

The job description is the foundation of the appointment process and should be prepared carefully. It should cover the following information: purpose of the job; main duties of the job; accountabilities and relationships; and any special circumstances or requirements. A summary of terms and conditions (salary scale, holidays, sick leave etc) should also be included. Box C provides a summary of the main elements of a job description.

Box C: Elements of a job description

Designation/title of post

Overall purpose/function of post
It is important to keep this brief. A useful rule of thumb is that, if the purpose cannot be summarised in one sentence, you are probably describing more than one job.

Key duties
These should be as clear and specific as possible. Duties should be listed in order of importance and distinguish between essential and occasional or secondary tasks.

Main relationships and accountabilities
- **To whom responsible**
  You may need to distinguish between day-to-day accountability to a line manager and overall accountability to the management committee.
- **For whom responsible**
  Even if workers have no responsibility for paid staff, they may be responsible for the coordination and support of volunteers.
- **Significant relationships**
  These may include relationships within the project (for example, reporting back to a particular committee) and those beyond the project (for example, liaison with a local community forum).

Special circumstances or requirements (not comprehensive)
- **Duration of post**
  State the duration of the post you are offering.

- **Unsocial hours**
  Many community projects do not operate nine to five: state whether evening or weekend working is involved on either a regular or an occasional basis.
- **Travel**
  If travel is an essential part of the post, this needs to be specified.

Terms and conditions (not comprehensive)
- **Scale/grade/salary range**
  Local voluntary organisations commonly use the salary scales set out in the Local Authorities National Joint Council Agreements (referred to as NJC scales), obtainable from local authority personnel officers or the Local Government Management Board*. These are subject to an annual pay award and, ideally, workers on these scales should also receive annual incremental increases within their specified grade. However, only commit to what your budget can afford. Note that grading should be determined by the responsibilities of the post and not the job title. For part-time posts, specify the number of hours and cite the scale pro rata.
- **Hours of work**
  State whether full-time or part-time.
- **Holiday entitlement**
  For part-time posts, arrange on a pro rata basis and express as working days.
- **Flexitime/time off in lieu/cover arrangements**
- **Sick leave arrangements**

How do you determine the key duties of a post? A start is to think about what you want to achieve by the end of your funding. What is your project worker working towards? Thinking about the overall purpose and direction of the post will enable you to determine the individual tasks necessary to achieve this goal.

Next, consider the role of the worker in the process: which of the tasks you have identified could be the worker's sole responsibility; which could be shared with the management committee or volunteers; and which could be delegated? Volunteers and management committees may be tempted to drop their responsibilities once a worker is in post.

Thinking about the worker's role within the project will help you to clarify his or her contribution more precisely, thereby ensuring that your project benefits from the specialist skills you are paying for.

Finally, think about the length of the working week and check that time and resources allocated are sufficient to carry out all tasks identified. It is especially important to do this for part-time posts, where the unconscious expectation of the employer, and perhaps the worker, is that full-time responsibilities can be completed in part-time hours. If you find that your list is too ambitious, consider dropping or reassigning any task that does not relate directly to your goals.

Note that a job description, once drawn up and agreed, has a function beyond the recruitment process. It will form part of your legal contract with the worker and may be used to monitor and review the worker's performance on the job. Since most jobs change over time, it is advisable to include within the job description some provision for amendments. This may happen either as a result of an annual review (which may reveal an over-ambitious workload) or a change in external circumstances resulting in new or increased responsibilities for the worker. Since the post you are advertising is likely to be new, provision for flexibility is essential. Remember that you cannot alter a job description unilaterally: any significant amendments must be mutually agreed.

Person specification

Now that you have determined the key tasks of the job, you will need to draw up a person specification. Its purpose is to define the criteria by which a candidate's experience, knowledge, skills and attitudes are judged adequate and appropriate for the job you have designed. A secondary benefit of preparing a person specification is that, even before you get to selection, you have set in place a means by which to assess the relative merits of different candidates.

The person specification lends objectivity to a highly subjective exercise. However, even when drawn up with careful attention to equal opportunities issues, the criteria chosen can reveal assumptions: for example, including leisure interests within your criteria may open the way to an unconscious bias towards middle-class lifestyles. Consequently, you are recommended to employ a more 'bias-free' set of categories for judging candidates. The types of headings used currently are:

- Skills (e.g. training)
- Knowledge (e.g. child protection legislation)
- Experience (e.g. management of volunteers)
- Qualifications (e.g. qualification in youth and community work)
- Qualities/values (e.g. commitment to equal opportunities)
- Other requirements (e.g. willingness to work unsocial hours)

It is now common to make parallel lists of 'essential' and 'desirable' characteristics under each of these general headings. For example, if you are advertising for the coordinator of an after-school club, experience of working within a similar project might be desirable, but experience of working with children in either a paid or a voluntary capacity would be essential. Avoid over-defining the basic requirements and ensure that your 'essential' characteristics contain only the minimum necessary to do the job. If you are unsure, a useful guideline is to ask whether a particular characteristic is something you need to have or would merely be beneficial. Inclusion of the latter as essential may prevent capable applicants from coming forward.

You may wish to ensure that your person specification is written in such a way as to encourage applications from sections of the community who are able to do the job, but might not necessarily apply. You should not specify either sex or race unless the job requires a particular type of person for reasons of decency or authenticity. For example, a domestic refuge may require a woman worker and a club for young African-Caribbean boys may require a black worker. In such circumstances, the sex or race of the worker is considered to be a genuine occupational qualification (GOQ), but you should be aware that GOQs can only apply to the filling of a job or training for a job. Plus, in order to ensure that they are not used to circumvent anti-discriminatory practice, the circumstances in which a GOQ applies are strictly defined.

A related issue, important for church groups, is whether or not the post-holder should be a Christian. It is not discriminatory in itself to make 'Christian' a necessary condition of being appointed to a job. There are some posts—for example, an evangelist—for which this would be an essential requirement. On the other hand, if you are hoping to appoint a manager to develop the church premises for community use, does the same requirement fall into the 'essential' or 'desirable' category? Here you will need to check that your decision does not discriminate against some sections of the community and that it can be justified. If there is no necessary religious link—for example, where the manager's post is seen primarily in relation to the community rather than as part of Christian witness—a decision to restrict the post to Christians may be illegal. You will also need to weigh up whether the 'gain' of a Christian worker is outweighed by the 'loss' of the opportunity to select from a broader field. This issue may have financial implications, as some funders cannot support posts that are not open to all.

Having considered the issues carefully, you may still decide that a Christian worker is a priority for your project. You are within your rights to do this, but in the interests of community relations this requirement should be tactfully worded. Many church projects prefer to state their value basis and activities, followed by the requirement that 'candidates must be in sympathy with the aims of the project'. In any post you must be clear whether the post is open to all and what, if any, religious criteria are to be used. You must also be able to justify your decision and to demonstrate consistent application of the criteria throughout your appointment process.

Designing an application form

It may be tempting to skip this task and ask applicants to submit a *curriculum vitae*. There are, however, strong arguments in favour of the standard application form from both the applicant's and the employer's perspective. In the former case, the applicant has a much clearer idea of what is required and does not have to second guess what you are looking for. Meanwhile, you are able to determine what information is given; you can locate and compare information more easily; and you have clarified in advance issues to address at interview. Moreover, now that you have clarified the experience and skills you need through the process of drawing up your job description and person specification, the task of designing an application form should be straightforward.

In order to avoid conscious and unconscious prejudices, the personal circumstances of applicants should not be taken into account. This means that there are some questions you should never ask on an application form. To give a very clear example, do not include a question about trade union membership, since failure to appoint on this basis is unlawful. Medical questions should be addressed to both sexes and phrased neutrally: e.g. 'How many days have you had off sick in the past twelve months?' not 'Are you able to carry out your normal duties during your monthly period?' You should also avoid asking for *any* information about marital status or children, which may be seen as discriminatory. The Equal Opportunities Commission* recommends that all such questions be removed from application forms. If you need such information for monitoring purposes, the questions should be asked on a separate sheet which is not available to those involved in selection. If the

---

Box D: Elements of an application form

Personal information
- name (ask for first or forename rather than Christian name)
- title
- address
- telephone numbers (home and work)

Education and qualifications
Give opportunity to include vocational training and in-service courses.

Present and previous employment

Other relevant experience
For example, voluntary work.

Christian experience/church involvement
If relevant to the post.

Personal statement
- health
- illnesses
- registered disabilities
- criminal offences (essential if post involves work with vulnerable groups)

Work permit requirements

Driving licence
If essential to the job, ask for details of any endorsements.

Period of notice required

Referees
- name
- contact information
- title and/or relationship with applicant
- employer (ask when you may contact current employer)
- minister/church member (if Christian experience or church involvement is relevant to the post)

Declaration of accuracy of information
To be signed by applicant.

You may also decide to include a detachable equal opportunities form together with an explanation of the purpose and use of this information.

information is needed later either for tax purposes or for your personnel records, ask only after the process has been completed.

A more positive approach is to look at the application form as a way of demonstrating your commitment to equal opportunities: remember that your recruitment documentation represents your project to the wider public and that evidence of good practice is likely to attract like-minded applicants. In addition to avoiding discriminatory or potentially discriminatory questions, use your form to encourage the widest possible range of applications. The detachable monitoring form described above, especially if accompanied by an explanation of its purpose and use, is one method.

You may also include a section on the application form which encourages applicants to relate life experience to the demands of the job. This particularly benefits those who have had fewer educational or employment opportunities, but may have much to offer the job.

The application form, together with the job description and person specification, completes the core documentation of your application pack. In order to assist enquirers with their applications (especially those who do not know the project or area), you are recommended to add some information about your project: a single sheet describing its background, context and future development is usually enough, but you may also wish to include your equal opportunities statement, leaflets and newsletters.

A covering letter should state the deadline for applications and the date of shortlisting and interviews. If you intend to contact only those applicants who make the shortlist, it is courteous to inform applicants of this: 'if you have not heard from us by [date], please assume that on this occasion your application has been unsuccessful'. Note that application packs should be compiled before your advertisement appears: this ensures that all essential information is ready for sending out and that enquirers have maximum time to consider the material.

Advertising

Now that you know what you need, how do you ensure that you attract the required skills and experience? The classified advertisement is not the only way to fill a vacancy: an estimated 60 to 80 per cent of vacancies are filled via 'informal market' processes of contacts, networking and cold calls.

Given the cost of advertising and the possibility that people have already expressed interest in your post, advertising your new post by informal methods such as 'word of mouth' may appeal. It is perfectly acceptable to make people aware that you are looking for staff. You should be aware that recruitment conducted entirely on this basis may result in claims of discrimination if it reduces the opportunity for all races and both sexes to apply. ACAS* considers that, 'this recruitment method should not be used where the workforce is wholly or predominantly white or black and the labour market is multi-racial.' In addition to demonstrating your commitment to equal opportunities, an advertisement will attract a wider range of applicants from which to choose.

You will find a brief summary of the important elements of an advertisement in Box E. However, you must still decide where to advertise and this will depend on a variety of factors. A practical consideration is cost: many voluntary organisations, including community projects, advertise jobs in *The Guardian* on Wednesdays, but such advertisements are expensive (and shortlisted candidates are also likely to have higher interview expenses).

You will need to weigh up whether the post you are offering (particularly if part-time, very short-term or modestly paid) justifies the expense of a national

Box E: Elements of a job advertisement

Content
The text should be genuinely informative, but not too full to cramp the overall effect. It should include the following basic information:

- the name of your organisation
- the name of the post
- brief description of job and location
- main skills and qualifications required
- full-time or part-time hours
- salary or salary scale (state pro rata if part-time)
- duration of post (state if this is determined by a specific grant)
- contact information for further information and application forms
- closing date for applications
- interview date
- statement about equal opportunities policy
- statement of exemption under relevant legislation (if a GOQ applies)

Design
Your headline should be large and eye-catching. If your project's name is not likely to be known to potential applicants put the job title in the heading where it may be more effective.

Think carefully about what will have primary importance in the heading and the text—for example, job, interest, pay, opportunities, location.

If your project has a logo or motif, this can add to the impact of the advertisement. Some funders require their logo to be used on an advertisement for any post supported by their money.

advertisement. Generally speaking, only jobs that require specialist qualifications or a wide range of experience should be advertised via national publications. If you are keen to encourage applications from minority ethnic groups, advertising nationally via *The Voice* is a good investment.

If national advertising is not appropriate to the post or your budget, you still have access to a wide range of free or low-cost alternatives. In addition to local newspapers (including free papers) and the internal newsletters of community or voluntary organisations, you will find that the local edition of *The Big Issue* advertises a range of 'people' jobs. If it is important that the person you appoint is a Christian, you may also wish to target denominational newspapers or newsletters of ecumenical networks. Many denominational and magazines are published weekly, others are published on a monthly basis. The internal newsletters of some of the most relevant ecumenical networks, for example, *CCWA News* (Churches' Community Work Alliance*), may be published even less frequently. Consequently, if it is important to advertise widely in the Christian press and within relevant Christian organisations and networks, you may need to find out about publication dates and book advertising space at an even earlier stage than is usually recommended.

In addition to advertising via newspapers and newsletters, you might consider placing notices in job centres, community centres, churches and local shops. In order to ensure that anyone from any background has the opportunity to be aware of your job offer, make sure you do this systematically: for example, if you are circulating posters around local churches, make sure that majority black churches are included. Local radio provides an alternative to print and may reach an even wider section of the community. It is also possible to advertise posts via community websites, but in view of the fact that access to the Internet is still limited, this should not be the sole method.

2.3 Selecting what you need

In the next phase of the appointment process you must first decide which applicants to interview and then who from this group is to be offered the job. If you receive more applications than you expect, this task may appear daunting. But take heart from the fact that your careful preparatory work is about to pay dividends. The basis of your decision-making at both the shortlisting and interview stages will be the criteria you have already identified.

Shortlisting

You should begin this task as soon as possible after the closing date for applications. Every member of your group should have copies of all completed application forms. These should be read through before starting to shortlist: you may decide to distribute these before you meet to allow more time for members to consider each application carefully. Shortlisting should be undertaken by the group, which should aim to arrive at a consensus of opinion on an absolute maximum of six names. You should aim, ideally, for a shortlist of no less than three and no more than five candidates. Whichever way you run the process, it is essential that it is fair.

What does this mean in practice? First, only information contained in the application form should be considered. If a volunteer who already works for the project and has appropriate experience and skills applies for the post, but provides no supporting evidence in her application, she cannot be selected. This may be frustrating if you are convinced of her potential to do the job. However, to make exceptions or allowances for applicants who are known to the project would disadvantage others.

Second, your main guide in shortlisting is the essential and desirable criteria set out under each category of your person specification. You will need to check each application against each criterion: on the basis of this analysis you may decide to eliminate any which do not meet the essential criteria.

Bear in mind that, on the basis of the application form, it is only really possible to determine whether applicants have the required skills, knowledge, qualifications and experience to do the job. 'Softer' criteria, such as applicants' values and personal qualities, are better tested at interview. Consequently, you may prefer to use the criteria as a basis for scoring each application according to the evidence provided in the application form: the six highest scores determine who is to be interviewed.

Shortlisted applicants should be contacted immediately after your meeting. This should be by letter stating the date and time of the interview; the venue and travel directions; arrangements for paying interview expenses; the interview format and any special tasks expected of the candidate (e.g. a presentation). Applicants should be asked to confirm attendance with a named individual as soon as possible and full contact details should be provided.

If there is likely to be a delay in sending out this letter or if the time between shortlisting and interview is unavoidably short, you may wish to communicate this information by telephone in advance. If so, make sure that you communicate the same information to all candidates on the same day. If you did not inform applicants of an intention to contact shortlisted candidates only, you should also write to those who have not been successful.

Interviewing

Interviews are a two-way process: you are selecting your worker and the candidate decides whether or not to accept the job. The onus is on you to conduct the process in a way that demonstrates the professionalism of your project and treats each candidate fairly and with respect.

This does not always happen—'chaotic', 'run by people who weren't properly briefed', 'bored', 'drunk', 'muddled me up with another candidate'—are some criticisms made of interview processes and panels. Such negative experiences are likely to damage the reputation of your project and deter candidates from accepting a job offer. With careful preparation and an orderly, thorough approach to each stage of the task, even first-time interviewers can avoid the worst pitfalls. The following guidelines for the preparation and conduct of the interview will serve as the basis for your own process.

Before the interview

- Draw up a programme for the day in order to plan the timing: a rough estimate is 30 to 45 minutes for each interview plus 10 to 15 minutes for writing notes. If you have asked candidates to make a presentation, you need to allow for this. Remember that your programme should include sufficient time for candidates to look around, to get a feel for the project and—if possible—to meet some of the people they will be working with
- Ensure that the interview room is in a part of the building where you will be undisturbed by other users and telephone calls. It should be clean and welcoming and neither too stuffy nor too cold
- Avoid 'inquisitorial' furniture arrangements—e.g. seating the candidate on a low chair or directly opposite a full interviewing panel. It is a good idea to have glasses and water available for both the candidates and the selection panel
- Arrange for candidates to be met at reception, preferably by someone who is not part of the selection panel. It is a good idea to ask this person to take responsibility for dealing with candidates' expenses and for looking after candidates during the process. Do not underestimate the importance of this role. Well-cared-for candidates are more likely to perform well, accept an offer and carry away a good impression of your project
- Plan your questions. These should be designed to probe candidates' knowledge, abilities and attitudes and relate to the criteria you have already identified. Other questions should be aimed at a more general assessment: do not ask for personal information or views which are irrelevant to the job. If—and only if—the post requires a personal commitment to the Christian faith, you may explore this further
- Decide who is to chair and lead the interviews. Allocate your questions to different members of the panel. It is good practice to ask all candidates the same questions in the same order. However, you may need to adapt the wording to reflect different experiences: questions about 'your current job' are unlikely to bring out the best in candidates who are not in paid employment
- Draw up an interview report form for each member of the interviewing panel. This should include a complete list of questions, space for notes of candidates' answers and a score (usually 1 to 5) for each answer. In note-taking, focus on the evidence that the candidate fulfills the person specification

During the interview

- Begin slowly and carefully—it takes time for candidates (and inexperienced interviewers) to settle down. Introduce everyone on the interviewing panel and give some background information about the project and the job involved
- Make the candidate feel at ease—aggressive interviewing is not likely to reveal the candidate's best qualities. Outline the purpose, length and structure of the interview and explain any note-taking procedures to be used. You may also state that there will be an opportunity to ask questions
- It is helpful to begin with questions which are immediately familiar to the candidate, such as the relevance of his/her present experience to the post, before working backwards to previous experience and finally forwards to the candidate's ideas about the job you are offering
- Open-ended questions ('tell us what you think about...') encourage the candidate to speak freely, since they cannot be answered by yes or no
- Once the candidate is at ease, you can follow up open-ended questions by some which oblige him/her to express a positive opinion
- Interviewers should avoid expressing their own views—to keep the interview flowing, use encouraging gestures. If you want to find out more, you may within equal opportunities guidelines to ask supplementary questions (for clarification or to probe) on a particular topic
- You are obliged by law not to discriminate on grounds of gender, marital status, race and disability. But you also need to be aware of personal prejudices, e.g. for or against fat people, suede shoe wearers, 'public school' accents, which stand in the way of sound judgement
- Allow time for candidates to ask questions and encourage them to do so. These may be revealing and helpful. You should anticipate the information needed to meet the more likely ones (for example, training opportunities or support structures)
- Keep track of time and ensure that essential points are covered. Ensure you can check the time without looking at a wrist watch
- Check that the candidate is familiar with the full terms and conditions of employment and that these are acceptable. Asking candidates whether they would accept the post if offered will assist the decision-making process

- Tell the candidate at the end of the interview when and how they may expect to hear the panel's decision

At the end of long and tiring day—interviewing is tiring—you may be keen to come to a decision quickly. However, in view of the effort you have invested in the process, decision-making should not be rushed. You may find yourself in unanimous agreement on the candidate you want (or, alternatively, on any candidate whom you would definitely not wish to appoint). It may also be that the 'right candidate' is not so obvious and your decision will involve weighing up and balancing a range of different factors.

Whatever position you find yourself in, your task is to make an assessment of each candidate against the criteria set out in the person specification. You are not judging candidates against each other. It is important that decisions are based on the evidence each panel member has gathered from the interview (your notes and scores). The process of conferring and matching evidence against criteria will ensure that an 'obvious decision' is firmly based. It will also serve as a necessary check against subjective impressions which may, for example, favour a candidate with an attractive personality above a quieter candidate with a stronger track record.

The procedures you have put in place will safeguard your decision-making against discrimination and over-subjectivity. You still need to bear in mind that interviews are not an exact science. Agreement on who should be offered the job should be reached by consensus, but sometimes panels may consider all the evidence and still disagree on which candidate should be offered the job, perhaps because more than one candidate meets all the criteria you have set. In such situations you may opt for a vote. To ensure confidence and backing for the appointment, all members of the panel must agree to support the decision and maintain confidentiality.

Note that, although you may encourage under-represented groups to apply for the post, positive action is not permissible at the selection stage. You should not at this stage decide against, say, a male candidate on the basis that 'we really need a woman in the team'.

It is better to take a break, even sleep on it, than to decide on grounds other than merit. Alternatively, you might ask each member of the panel to write down their assessment and then pool all views: this strategy is a useful way of checking whether one member's preference is over-influencing the panel.

It may be that no candidate emerges as suitable and you decide not to make an appointment. This can be frustrating and disappointing for all involved. But the extra time and expense of re-advertising need to be weighed against the consequences of appointing a worker who would not be competent or happy in the job, which will prove expensive in the long-term. If you do find yourself in this situation, try to be positive: use the interview as an opportunity to review the way in which the post was drawn up and advertised. Your job description may have been unrealistic, or your advertising strategy either too limited or poorly positioned.

The actions you should take in relation to your successful candidate are described in the next section. In the euphoria of arriving at a decision, do not forget the unsuccessful candidates. Although it is not always practical to write to non-shortlisted candidates once a post has been accepted by either your first or second choice, you should contact all those you have interviewed. Be prepared for requests for feedback. To avoid difficulties and to ensure that your answers are honest and constructive, you may wish to have the interview notes to hand when you make the call. These will ensure that your feedback is based on evidence measured against the criteria set out in the person specification. You should follow up your telephone call to each candidate with a letter thanking them for their interest.

2.4 Securing your worker

The aim of the final stage in the appointment process is to secure your worker. Tasks include making a job offer; obtaining references; conducting essential checks; and drawing up a contract of employment. A contract, strictly speaking, does not have to be provided before the worker is in post. However, since there is a close connection between the contract and the duties, terms and conditions set out in the job description, it is helpful to consider the contract within the context of the appointment process. Please note that legal advice is beyond the scope of this introductory guide.

Making a job offer

Now that you have decided on a candidate (preferably with a second choice in case your preferred candidate refuses the offer), you will need to act quickly. It is possible that the person you want has other irons in the fire and delay at this stage could lose you your worker. You should telephone the successful candidate as soon as possible in order to confirm whether the person will accept the post. If yes, request permission to take up references.

Although a verbal offer is legally binding, candidates are unlikely to resign their current posts until a written offer is received. Your telephone call should therefore be followed by a letter, first class post, the same or following day, making a written offer. It should confirm the starting date, the starting salary and any conditions (offers may be subject to references, checks, probationary periods etc). It should also request confirmation in writing as soon as possible and copies of any documentation that may be needed.

Checks and references

Best practice recommends that references should only be taken up after an offer has been made. You should request permission to do this in the letter with the conditional offer of employment: no references should be sought from a current employer without the applicant's permission. Make sure that you send a job description and a person specification with a request for a written reference, as this will give the referee a better idea of the kind of information you need. A stamped addressed envelope should also be included.

In addition to references, you may need to conduct essential checks. If the post involves substantial unsupervised access to children and young people under 18 or other vulnerable groups, you should be sure to check the chosen candidate's criminal background. To verify the declaration in the application form, police checks should be made. The Department of Health currently provides a vetting service (for which a charge may be made).

The candidate's declaration in the application form should be a sufficient indicator of health, but some employers may wish to go further. If so, a decision to request a full medical examination should be based only on the duties of the post, not on the perceived capacity of the worker. You may, therefore, check the health of a candidate whose duties will involve heavy physical work. You should not request a check on the grounds that your chosen candidate has a disability. Note that you must pay the cost of any medical examination and that medical details must remain confidential.

Finally, you should be aware that it is a criminal offence to employ a person who is not entitled to work in the UK. Employers committed to equal opportunities may feel uncomfortable with this. If a check is conducted systematically, if the candidate knows what documents they are expected to produce and when, and you treat all documents as having equal status, your procedure need not be seen as discriminatory.

Any document showing name and National Insurance number will usually cover most employees: passports, birth certificates and letters from the Home Office are also acceptable documentation. You will find comprehensive guidance on this issue in a free Home Office publication, *Guidance for Employers: Prevention of Illegal Working* (available via helpline 020 8649 7878).

Drawing up a contract of employment

It may come as a surprise to learn that you have no obligation to provide your worker with a contract of employment. On the other hand, any employee who joins your project for one month or more (unless employed for fewer than eight hours per week) is entitled to a written statement setting out the main terms and conditions of their employment. This must be provided within two months of starting work, but it is good practice to ensure that your worker has access to a written statement of terms and conditions from day one. Please note that the written statement only informs employees of the general terms of a contract: it forms a major part of the contract, but not all of it. Job descriptions, letters of appointment, grievance procedures—even promises made in conversation—may also be considered as terms of the contract. Although you have no legal obligation to provide a contract of employment, many organisations find it simpler to issue a contract which incorporates the statement of terms and conditions you are obliged by law to provide. These are listed as mandatory requirements in

---

Box F: Elements of a contract of employment

Mandatory requirements (which must be stated in full)
- the name of the employer and employee
- the job title and summary of duties (detail may be given in job description)
- the place of work (state if worker will be required to work elsewhere)
- the date of commencement of continuous employment
- rate of remuneration (and interval of payment)
- termination of contract (include notice period and duration of contract if fixed-term)
- hours of work (include normal working hours; any requirement to work outside these hours; flexi-time arrangements etc.)
- statement of trade union recognition or non-recognition
- holiday entitlement and pay

Mandatory requirements (which may be detailed separately)
- grievance procedure
- disciplinary procedure
- any pension provisions
- sickness entitlement and pay

Non-mandatory requirements (which it may be sensible to include)
- maternity leave
- extended maternity absence
- maternity pay
- contractual maternity leave and pay
- parental leave
- other leave (e.g. compassionate leave)
- variation of contract
- part-time employees
- equal opportunities
- health and safety
- probationary period

Signatures
- employee's
- employer's representative on behalf of named project

Box F. Note that not every mandatory requirement needs to be set out in full: grievance and disciplinary procedures, for example, could either be issued separately or as part of a staff handbook. NCVO* suggests that small organisations may find it easier to have most of their terms and conditions set out in one place.

You will find sample contracts of employment included in many of the publications listed in Appendix A: NCVO* has also produced a comprehensive free leaflet, *Contract of Employment. Standard Terms and Explanatory Notes*, which is available from the Legal Team.

Whatever model you choose, the contract you intend to issue must be developed with the specific needs and resources of your project in mind. It is not responsible practice to offer benefits beyond your budget.

Equally, you should avoid committing the project's management committee to lengthy or cumbersome procedures—such as consultation with trade unions prior to redundancies—if they cannot practically be implemented.

Another issue to bear in mind when looking at sample contracts is that employment legislation is continually developing: you need to anticipate any developments which are likely to impact upon your practice. For example, in order to avoid claims of unfair dismissal from a worker reaching the end of a fixed-term contract, a well-established precaution taken by many voluntary sector and other employers has been the insertion of a so-called 'waiver' clause into the contract of employment. However, under the Employment Relations Bill (1999), with effect from 25 October 1999, the use of waiver clauses on unfair dismissal has been declared illegal. They may, however, legitimately be used to avoid claims for redundancy payments: you will find more information on waiver clauses in Section 4.

Finally, you should never forget that a contract is a legally binding document. If either employer or employee breaches any of the provisions—that is, breaks the agreement between them—you may have a case for legal action. Consequently, if you are in doubt about the implications of any terms, take advice before using them. In any case, you should always ensure that any contract of employment is read through and checked before it is issued.

Checklist

The following questions are designed to encourage your group to think through the appointment process.

✔ Are you satisfied that the legal structure of your project is appropriate to your new responsibilities?

✔ Have you decided which groups and people need to be represented on your working group? What skills and experience do you require? Who will be responsible for which task?

✔ Have you drawn up a timetable for the process? Is it realistic? Have you allowed flexibility?

✔ Have you clarified the main aim of the post? What is to be the contribution of the worker to the project? What specific tasks need to be included in the job description so that your goals can be achieved?

✔ Is the working group clear about the criteria for selection? If you intend to specify a GOQ and/or religious criterion, can these be justified by the nature of the work involved?

✔ Is your application form designed to enable assessment of the criteria you have identified in the person specification? Have you checked that it is free of discriminatory and/or irrelevant personal questions?

✔ Has your advertising strategy been developed with reference to equal opportunities, the budget for the appointment process and advertisers' deadlines?

✔ How will the shortlisting and interviewing panels be briefed on the criteria for selection?

✔ Which, if any, additional checks may be needed before you confirm a job offer? How do you intend to ensure that the procedure is non-discriminatory?

✔ Does the written statement of terms and conditions/contract of employment you intend to issue fulfil all the legal requirements? If you wish to go beyond the legal minimum, have you checked that your project is able to deliver?

✔ If you decide not to make an appointment, what is to be learned from the experience?

3 Working

Unlike the process of making an appointment, which follows a particular order, setting up appropriate structures to support the worker on the job is less straightforward. Consequently, five 'issue clusters' are considered in this section: financial responsibilities; health and safety issues; disciplinary and grievance procedures; monitoring and assessment; and support and development.

Issues covered in the first three, such as a system for dealing with income tax, are mainly legal requirements which you will need to have in place by the time the worker is in post. Those in the last two clusters, which include issues such as training, are optional requirements, but can contribute to the development of your work. As with other optional requirements, you need to take time to think through what your project can realistically offer. Remember also that the principle of equal opportunities must inform the development of your policies and procedures: benefits and sanctions in employment must apply to all.

3.1 Financial responsibilities

Neglect of any of the issues considered under this heading will result in considerable difficulties for the worker and, in a worst case scenario, legal action against the employer. Ignorance of the law is no excuse. It is therefore important, especially if you have no previous experience in this area, to research your responsibilities thoroughly. Please note that only a brief introduction to each issue is given: for comprehensive and up-to-date information and advice, you must consult the relevant authorities.

Pay
In the process of making your appointment you will have decided upon an appropriate rate of pay. Having advertised the post and made an offer based on this rate, you have a legal obligation to pay at the level agreed. Now that you have made an appointment, the next step is to set up the procedures by which your worker is to be paid.

This may appear obvious, but it is not unknown for the task to be overlooked. A community worker, appointed by a newly-formed ecumenical body, reports, 'At the end of my first month I discovered that I hadn't been paid—everyone thought someone else was responsible, so I had to organise the cheque and ring round the management committee to get it signed.' Negligence resulting in inconvenience and stress for your worker is a sure way to damage a new working relationship.

Your first step must be to assign responsibility for dealing with the payment of wages and salaries. The simplest option, especially if only one worker is involved, is to identify someone within the management committee with an interest and expertise in project finance.

If nobody has the confidence or experience to take on this role, you may prefer to assign the task elsewhere. For example, it is sometimes possible to arrange payment through the structures of your denomination—at least one Church of England diocese organises the payment of project workers centrally—but this arrangement is unusual. Alternatively, you might consider using a payroll bureau. Some local authorities, Councils for Voluntary Service and community accountancy projects offer a low-cost service to projects and small voluntary organisations. If none of these options is available, you can use a commercial payroll bureau (usually listed under payroll services in *Yellow Pages*), but you must be prepared to pay commercial rates.

The frequency and method of payment will have been specified in the terms and conditions of appointment, so does not need to be discussed here. It is worth remembering that a common system of payment—monthly in arrears made directly into an employee's bank account—may not be the most appropriate to all circumstances and needs. As one manager of a project in an area with high unemployment found, 'You get a cleaner on maybe four pounds an hour, three hours a week—you want to pay them on a monthly basis, they want 12 quid a week.'

Whatever system of payment you agree, you must ensure that you keep adequate records and meet your responsibilities with regard to tax and National Insurance.

Income Tax and National Insurance
These become your responsibility if you make payments of any kind, such as a salary, overtime payments, bonuses, sick pay, one-off cash payments, which amount to more than the tax and National

Insurance threshold. It is therefore important to ask the local Inland Revenue* office for the address of your tax office as soon as you know that you are employing a worker. This will ensure that you are registered for a Pay As You Earn (PAYE) scheme, the system used for calculating and collecting Income Tax and Class 1 National Insurance Contributions (NICs) from payments made to your employees. Note that, in April 1999, the Contributions Agency merged with the Inland Revenue*. This means that the Inland Revenue now deals not only with income tax, but with NICs, Statutory Maternity and Sick Pay.

Once registered, you should receive a PAYE Reference Number, a payment book and an *Employer's Quick Guide to PAYE*. The guide will provide you with all the basic information you need to fulfil the following responsibilities:

- **Deducting the right amount of tax from pay**
  This is determined by several factors: your employee's tax code; the employee's level of entitlement to tax-free earnings; the gross amount earned since the beginning of the current tax year; the amount of taxable pay; the amount of tax already deducted; and the remaining tax due on the taxable pay. A worker moving to your project from another employer will provide information on tax status with a P45. If the worker cannot produce a P45, you should consult the employer's guide.
- **Working out the amount to be paid in National Insurance Contributions**
  Employees earning more than the lower earnings limit have to pay Class 1 NICs on all earnings up to the higher earnings limit. Employers must pay NICs on all earnings, however high the total, if the employee earns more than the lower earnings limit. Contribution tables are issued by the Inland Revenue Contributions Agency in March: note also that the lower and higher earnings limits are reviewed annually in April.
- **Keeping records of pay and deductions**
  It is advisable, especially if you hope to employ more workers, also to keep a separate wages book. The tax deductions working sheet (P11), which must be completed for each employee at the end of every month, is acceptable as a basic record. These should be kept for a minimum of six years after the end of the tax year to which they apply.
- **Paying the Inland Revenue amounts due monthly**
  Every month you must pay the Inland Revenue the total amount of tax deducted and the employer's and employees' NICs. These should be entered onto the employer's payment record (P32) and the amount due sent together with a payslip (P30B) to the Collector of Taxes within 14 days of the end of each tax month. If the amount of tax to be paid is low, employers may choose to pay quarterly (further information is available from the Inland Revenue).

- **Sending the Tax Office a return each tax year showing all payments and deductions**
  At the end of the tax year you should complete a form P14 for each person you have employed during the year. This three-part form, obtainable from the tax office, is basically a summary of the records on the P11. The first two sections of the P14 must be sent to the tax office together with form P35 (your employer's annual return listing all employees and their tax and NI records). The third section must be given to the employee and is somewhat confusingly then referred to as a P60.
- **Providing employees with records**
  Employees have a legal entitlement to a payslip giving details of the gross amount earned; the amounts of any variable or fixed deductions; and the net amount earned. (The Employment Rights Act (1996) prohibits any deductions from wages without the employee's consent.) They should also receive form P60 at the end of every tax year; form P11D if reimbursement of expenses applies; and form P45 upon leaving your employment. Further details are available from the Inland Revenue.

Pensions
Ideally, the cost of pension contributions should be taken into account at the fundraising stage, but an assessor for the National Lottery Charities Board doubts 'if one per cent of the bids I have seen contained any budget for pensions.' The poor performance of the voluntary sector in this area should not be used as an excuse to avoid making pension contributions. It is not only good practice to contribute, but also important to be prepared for any changes in legislation designed to force the hand of the reluctant employer. To use a related example, following a ruling from the European Court of Justice that part-time workers had the right to join occupational pension schemes, employers who had previously refused them access became liable for backdated claims.

NICs provide employees with a basic pension and the additional State Earnings Related Pension Scheme (SERPS). Since benefits given under SERPS are decreasing, employees can arrange to join a company pension scheme (which may be either contracted in or contracted out of SERPS) or to set up an additional personal pension. A third option is the new stakeholder pension plan, but full details of this scheme have not yet emerged.

Since the viability of a pension scheme depends on a critical mass of long-term contributors, it is not practical for a small project to set up its own company scheme. Projects can provide employees with occupational pensions without having to set up their own schemes. For example, voluntary organisations in receipt of funding from local authorities may have access to the Local Government Superannuation Scheme. If this does not apply to your project, you may find a suitable scheme via the Pensions Trust*, which provides different schemes for those in the voluntary sector and general welfare field. More recently, the trade union MSF* has pioneered the COVER pension scheme, which is available not just to union members but to all employees in the voluntary sector.

Your new worker may already have, or may wish to set up, a personal pension plan. The advantage of personal pension plans is that they are not affected by change of job and allow greater flexibility in the level of contributions. Consequently, despite their much-publicised disadvantages, they may be the best choice for employees on fixed-term contracts. They should, however, be encouraged to seek advice. If a personal pension does appear to be the best option, employers may contribute to personal pension plans by paying a percentage of salary direct to the pension supplier.

Statutory Sick Pay/Statutory Maternity Pay
Your responsibilities to your worker in the event of sickness and pregnancy will have been addressed in the contract of employment. Note that, even if you wish to pay more than the minimum, the costs of introducing contractual sick and maternity pay over and above the statutory schemes must be carefully considered. It is not always possible for a small project to offer more—and irresponsible to make commitments beyond your capacity to deliver. In both areas, you must by law meet minimum standards.

All employees who earn more than the lower earnings limit for NICs and are employed on a contract for more than three months are entitled to Statutory Sick Pay (SSP) once they have been ill for more than four consecutive days. SSP is paid at a flat rate. Employers are responsible for payment for periods of four days or more up to a total of 28 weeks absence in any one period of incapacity for work. If SSP paid in a month exceeds 13 per cent of a employer's total gross NICs for that month, it is possible to claim financial assistance under the Percentage Threshold Scheme. You can obtain details of this scheme and further information on employers' obligations with regard to SSP from the Contributions Agency.

Women who have completed 26 weeks of continuous service and earn above the lower earnings limit for the payment of National Insurance qualify for up to 18 weeks of Statutory Maternity Pay (SMP).

A higher rate (90 per cent of earnings) is payable for the first six weeks and a lower rate for the remaining twelve weeks. Payment of SMP is the employer's responsibility, but you can obtain reimbursement via your National Insurance and tax payments. Information on SMP is available from the Contributions Agency, or in the free leaflet (PL958—*Maternity Rights—a Guide for Employers and Employees*) published by the Department of Trade and Industry*.

It is important to remember that your responsibilities towards a pregnant employee extend beyond pay. Other issues, such as health and safety, maternity leave, the right to return to work, must also be addressed. Should the situation arise in the course of your worker's period of employment, you can obtain specialist advice and help from official bodies and voluntary organisations such as, among others, the Maternity Alliance*.

3.2 Health and safety

Health and safety legislation is a complex, growing field. For further information and guidance you should consult your regional office of the Health and Safety Executive (HSE)*, the body legally responsible for the enforcement of health and safety legislation. It also produces a wide range of free and low cost information leaflets which advise on both employers' general responsibilities and any regulations relating to specific hazards.

The main item of legislation you should be aware of is the Health and Safety at Work Act (1974). It covers general duties regarding health and safety, and serves as a framework for the following six regulations on:

- the management of health and safety
- health, safety and welfare in the workplace
- manual handling
- display screens
- provision and use of work equipment
- personal protective equipment

The Act applies to virtually all workers and workplaces. It also covers health and safety duties towards, among others, volunteers, self-employed workers, contractors working on the premises and members of the general public. Although this brief summary focuses on duties towards your employees, your responsibilities under the Act are much broader.

Employer's responsibilities
The general theme of the Act is that the primary responsibility for doing what is needed to avoid accidents and occupational ill-health lies with those who create the risks. Consequently, the Act puts a number of general duties on employees as well as employers: it is the duty of all employees while at work to take reasonable care for their own and others' health and safety and to cooperate with the employer in providing a safe working environment.

The promotion of health and safety is a management responsibility. Employers have a duty to ensure the health and safety and welfare at work of all employees via a planned strategy; to allocate responsibilities; and to inform (and, where necessary, provide appropriate training for) their workers.

What does this mean in practice? Employers are not expected to guarantee total protection against all risks to workers (although, see below, you must provide insurance cover). They are considered to have a duty to take all 'reasonably practicable' steps to ensure the health, safety and welfare at work of all staff. Thus your duties as an employer will include:

- the provision and maintenance of machinery, equipment, appliances and systems of work that are safe and without risks to health
- the provision of arrangements for ensuring health and safety in relation to the use, transport and storage of any articles or substances
- the provision of information, instruction, training and supervision necessary to ensure workers' health and safety
- ensuring that access to, and exit from, the workplace is safe and without risk to health
- the maintenance of the workplace so that it is safe and carries no risk to workers' health
- the provision of a working environment that is safe, carries no risk to health and has adequate regard to workers' welfare.

Note that, although the law does not specify the standard of protection you should meet, certain activities (such as the provision of food) are governed by codes of practice which do set down standards.

Management of health and safety
Your responsibilities with regard to the management of health and safety are set out in the Management of Health and Safety at Work Regulations (1992), one of the six regulations established within the framework of the Health and Safety at Work Act.

Your first responsibility is to conduct a systematic risk assessment in order to identify potential dangers. This exercise not only protects the worker, but all project users and visitors. In order to be fully effective, it should be reviewed at least annually: if you have appointed a worker either to initiate new activities or to work with new groups, your assessment is likely to become outdated very soon.

You will find detailed guidance on how to conduct a risk assessment in *Management of Health and Safety at Work. Approved Code of Practice*, a publication of the HSE*. It lays down the following general guidelines:

First, your assessment must take account of both significant general hazards, such as a trailing electric cable in the office, and any that are specific to your project. For example, if a furniture repair project runs on the premises, you will need to pay special attention to hazards presented by the use and storage of tools.

Second, you should have particular regard to people who are likely to be most vulnerable to risk. For example, is the worker young and/or inexperienced? Is the worker likely to be alone in the building? Does the worker have a disability? If any of these circumstances apply, are any special provisions—e.g. a panic button or extra telephone—required?

Third, the assessment should identify existing precautionary measures, which might include the provision of information, instruction or training, or the establishment of procedures (for example, a fire drill). It must also monitor their effectiveness: if, say, an instruction not to block entrance and exit points is ignored, this also constitutes a hazard and must be included.

Fourth, you need to ask if you have done all that is 'reasonably practicable' to control hazards. Are there any additional steps that could be taken? In the case of specific activities, such as food provision, you also need to check whether recognised standards apply. You must meet any laid down by law.

Finally, although only employers of five or more workers are required to keep a written record of significant findings, it is good practice to do so.

Health and safety policies
In addition to taking practical steps to minimise risks, you should be aware that Section 2 of the Health and Safety at Work Act requires employers of five or more workers to prepare a written health and safety policy. If you employ part-time, temporary or casual staff, they are also included.

Even if you employ just one worker, remember that the Act extends the scope of health and safety legislation to all persons at work—i.e. volunteers and self-employed workers as well as employees. It also protects the health and safety of the general public, such as visitors to the project or contractors working on the premises, who may be affected by work activities. To protect their own interests, all projects, and certainly any that employ paid staff, should have a written health and safety policy. This must be regularly reviewed and communicated to staff.

Your health and safety policy does not need to be detailed, but should aim to communicate basic information about health and safety issues. It should state your commitment to following health and safety legislation; outline procedures for addressing hazards; and name the persons responsible for assessing hazards. Since employers have a legal obligation to communicate health and safety information, your statement must be brought to the attention of all employees (as should subsequent alterations or updates to the policy). It should emphasise the need for cooperation on the part of employees.

Guidance on what to include in your policy is given in Box G. When drawing up your policy, ensure that it is both realistic and relevant to your project's circumstances and resources. Remember, too, that you are committed to doing whatever you say that you will do. Well-intentioned but impractical promises may have unpleasant legal consequences.

Specific health and safety policies may be developed as an ongoing process to cover new regulations, issues and changes. For example, a children's play-scheme which has taken care to ensure that equipment and play area meet safety standards may also need to take on board regulations applying to the administrator's VDU. Specific policies, like your general statement, should address responsibility for the assessment, monitoring and reporting of hazards and the processes for developing further policy within the project.

Box G: Elements of a health and safety policy

- a statement of your commitment to health and safety and your obligation to employees
- identification of the person responsible for implementing health and safety policy
- location of first aid equipment
- identification of the person responsible for using first aid equipment
- details of the location and use of an accident book
- statement of staff responsibilities with regard to equipment and working environment
- reference to your fire procedures (which may be dealt with elsewhere)
- reference to any particular health hazard arising from you project's activities (for example, food hygiene)

Insurance
Once you begin to employ staff you are required, under the Employers' Liability (Compulsory Insurance) Act (1969), to have employer's liability insurance and to display the certificate of cover on your premises. This will provide cover if your worker suffers illness or injury as a result of their employment—for example, falling off a ladder while reaching for a file—and may be extended to other staff. If you are planning to employ more staff, or to use temporary workers (for example, to assist with a summer play-scheme), you must ensure that every person with a contract of employment is covered. A brief guide to your responsibilities under the Act is available from the HSE*, but you must consult a broker to obtain advice on the level of cover you need.

As you look at the insurance implications of taking on staff, you are advised to check whether other types of insurance cover are adequate. It is likely that you will have buildings insurance in place, but is your cover affected by any new activities taking place on the premises? The same applies to public liability insurance covering accidents to members of the public visiting your premises: if numbers or the range of activities on-site increase, your cover is likely to be affected. Public liability insurance may also be needed to protect volunteers or management committee members. To find out whether your insurance cover is adequate, consult your insurance broker for professional advice. Please note that, as with health and safety, the level of your cover should be regularly reviewed. If you do not inform your insurance company of changes affecting cover, you may find that your policy is invalidated.

3.3 Disciplinary and grievance procedures

It may be tempting to delay drawing up procedures for your project, but you are advised to do so quickly. If you have not already included disciplinary and grievance procedures in your written statement of terms and conditions of employment, you should draw them up in the early stage of the employment relationship and certainly before the end of any probationary period. This is not only because you have a legal obligation to provide your worker with details of both, but also because you need to have structures in place should 'teething troubles' escalate into an unexpected dispute. A fraught situation is not a good basis upon which to draw up project policy.
You should recognise that both disciplinary and grievance procedures have an equal opportunities dimension. The Commission for Racial Equality* recommends that, in applying disciplinary procedures, consideration should be given to the possible effect on behaviour of racial abuse or other racial provocation, to communication and comprehension difficulties and to differences in cultural background or behaviour. Equally, a grievance about discrimination or harassment should not be dismissed on the assumption that the complainant is likely to be 'over-sensitive'. You should take care to ensure that your procedures and practices are non-discriminatory.

Disciplinary procedure
If this is an issue with which you feel uncomfortable, you may find it helpful to consider the definition of a disciplinary procedure offered by ACAS*: 'the means by which rules are observed and standards are obtained.'

In other words, a disciplinary procedure exists to protect good practice within the project and to promote and support the required improvement by the worker. It enables you to balance different responsibilities as an employer: to treat staff fairly and to protect the best interests of the project and its users. Be aware that failure to observe procedure may prove costly: a worst case scenario is a procedural error which results in compensation for unfair dismissal, even though you have acted fairly. You should, when drawing up your disciplinary procedure, be careful to distinguish between minor disciplinary issues and gross misconduct. The former category includes unsatisfactory work performance and unsatisfactory behaviour, misconduct and negligence (e.g. poor time-keeping, unacceptable absence, minor breaches of health and safety procedures).

As far as possible, you should aim as a first step to deal with minor disciplinary issues informally, taking care to establish whether the problem really is a disciplinary matter. For example, poor performance may indicate a need for further training and the root of unauthorised absence may be a domestic or health problem.

If the informal approach does not solve the problem, it may be necessary to invoke the formal disciplinary procedure set out in Box H. You may also invoke the disciplinary procedure if there is misconduct or breach of rules which is too serious to be handled informally.

The second category of disciplinary issue, gross misconduct, is defined by ACAS* as 'misconduct serious enough to destroy the employment contract between employer and employee and make any further working relationship and trust impossible.'

It is not possible to provide an exhaustive list of offences constituting gross misconduct but, generally speaking, the charge should be restricted to very serious offences. Specific examples are:

- dishonesty
- theft
- fraud
- physical assault on another person
- threatening behaviour
- deliberate damage to company property
- incapacity as a result of alcohol and/or drugs
- negligence causing unacceptable loss, damage or injury
- gross insubordination
- sexual and/or racial harassment
- deliberate failure to implement equal opportunities policy
- abuse or deliberate disclosure of confidential information
- criminal acts occurring outside employment which impact upon employment

In view of the serious nature of a charge of gross misconduct, a separate disciplinary procedure is followed. A summary may be found in Box H.

If you decide to implement a disciplinary action, whether for a minor offence or gross misconduct, you must observe certain protocols. First, the employee should be kept fully informed of both the nature of the complaint and the fact that the procedure is a disciplinary one. (It is especially important to make this clear if you are moving from an informal to a formal disciplinary action). Second, you should act promptly: it is not acceptable to drag out the procedure. It may help to specify a timescale: for example, if an employee is suspended for gross misconduct, you should aim to hold an investigation within one working week. Thirdly, you should keep written records of discussions as well as letters, which should be shown to the employee before being filed. Finally, employees should be given full opportunity to state their case and be kept fully informed of their rights throughout the process: these include the right to appeal and the right to be accompanied in a disciplinary interview. The Employment Relations Bill (1999) grants employees the right to be accompanied by a trade union representative *even if the employee is not a union member.*

Grievance procedure

The procedure which allows you to take action against an employee should be balanced by a structure which allows workers to bring individual grievances to the attention of management. For example, your worker may wish to raise a serious objection about an aspect of the working environment or an unrealistic workload. In such instances a grievance procedure provides a mechanism by which to raise a complaint, to have it considered by management and to have the employer decide whether or not the complaint should be accepted. It is also a legal requirement.

In many small organisations, the appeals procedure set out in the disciplinary procedure doubles as a grievance procedure. ACAS* recommends that grievance procedures should be kept separate from appeals. In a small project, where resources are limited and roles overlap, such a separation may not be practical. You must decide what is most appropriate to your circumstances and will best promote efficient and fair problem resolution.

If you are drawing up a separate grievance procedure, the protocol outlined in relation to disciplinary action also applies. First, just as an employer must inform the employee that action is disciplinary, the employee must state clearly that they are invoking a formal grievance procedure. Second, the procedure should be conducted as speedily as possible. You should specify timescales for each stage in the process, but take care to ensure that they are realistic: do not commit yourself to a timetable that is impossible for you to meet. Third, at every stage, details of the complaint and steps taken to resolve the issue should be documented.

Finally, as with disciplinary procedures, the worker has the right to be accompanied at any interview concerning a grievance. Under the Employment Relations Bill (1999), in cases of serious grievance, the right to representation has been strengthened.

Box H: Elements of a disciplinary procedure

- **A statement of the purpose of the disciplinary procedure and the principles upon which the procedure is based**
  It is usually sufficient to specify the aim of speedy resolution of any problem area and the principle of fairness to all parties involved. However, you may also wish to set down the principles of workers' rights to representation and the right to appeal against decisions.
- **A statement of the scope of the procedure**
  In the interests of equal opportunities, a disciplinary procedure should apply to all employees—full-time, part-time, temporary, fixed-term workers. However, to avoid confusing disciplinary procedures with the probation process, you may prefer to specify 'employees who have successfully completed their probationary period.'
- **A statement of the occasions upon which the procedure will be implemented**
  You do not need to provide an exhaustive list of issues leading to disciplinary action: it is sufficient to state that it 'will be taken where an employee's work, conduct or action warrants such a measure.'
- **A description of the procedure**
  Disciplinary procedures operate in stages, which may vary—an alternative to the procedure outlined below is two verbal warnings, followed by a written warning, followed by a final warning, followed by the final sanction of dismissal. However, at every stage it is important to specify the problem; the action required; a timetable for improvement; how improvement is to be measured (and by whom); and the consequences of a failure to improve. You should also specify what support has been offered.

  Stage 1 (Verbal warning) applies in the case of a minor offence. This should specify the reason for the warning, the status of the warning and inform the employee of his or her right to appeal. Brief notes may be kept on the employee's file, but you should also state when they may be disregarded.

  Stage 2 (Written warning) applies in the case of a more serious offence or if a previous offence (for which a verbal warning has been given) is repeated. It should also state the reason for the warning, a timescale for improvement and notification of the consequences of no improvement in this period.

  Stage 3 (Final written warning) applies in the case of further misconduct and should specify that a failure to improve will lead to dismissal. Once again, the worker should be informed of the right to appeal.

  Stage 4 (Termination) applies if there is insufficient improvement after a final written warning. If this decision is taken, the employee should be provided with written reasons for dismissal, the date of termination of employment and the right of appeal. A written statement of reasons for dismissal has been the legal entitlement of all employees with two years service, but with effect from 1 June 1999, an employee may make a request for written reasons for dismissal if they have been employed continuously for one year.

- **A statement of the procedure to be undertaken in cases of gross misconduct**
  You should, as far as possible, specify what you mean by gross misconduct. In order to cover all eventualities, you should make it clear that the list is not exhaustive and that other serious offences may also be included. It is usual, in such cases, to suspend the worker on full pay while the problem is investigated. If the investigation confirms the charge, the penalty is normally summary dismissal without payment or payment in lieu of notice.
- **An outline of the procedures to be followed if the employee wishes to appeal**
  Specify the time limit within which appeals at any stage in the disciplinary procedure must be lodged; where appeals are to be directed; and how they should be made (verbally or in writing). You should provide for an appeal to be heard as speedily as is practical. Ideally, it should be heard by an authority higher than the person taking the disciplinary action (i.e. the chair of the management committee rather than the line manager), but in a small project this distinction may not be easy to make. The decision of an appeals committee (which may consist of a full meeting of the management committee) is final. In the event of dismissal, an employee continuously employed for one year may bring a complaint of unfair dismissal before an Employment Tribunal.

As with disciplinary issues, efforts should be made to resolve a complaint informally. If this proves unsatisfactory, the formal grievance procedure may be invoked. This usually has fewer stages than a disciplinary procedure:

Stage 1: The worker should raise a complaint verbally with the person to whom the worker is accountable on a day-to-day basis. Should the line manager be the source of the complaint, you may wish to assign responsibility for grievance matters to another member of the management committee.

Stage 2: If the complaint is not resolved within the agreed timescale, it should be raised with the person to whom the worker has overall accountability (such as the chair of the management committee). You may wish to specify at this point that, from Stage 2, complaints should be written.

Stage 3: If still unresolved within the agreed timescale, the issue should be referred to the full management committee. A special meeting to resolve the situation should be held within an agreed period. Your timescale should have regard to the practicalities of arranging a meeting, as well as the need for prompt action.

The decision made at the last stage of the internal process should be regarded as final. If still unsatisfied, the worker may have recourse to an outside body such as ACAS* for advice and assistance.

3.4 Monitoring and assessment

Your legal obligation to draw up disciplinary and grievance procedures does not imply that these are the only means by which workplace issues should be addressed. If you establish good monitoring procedures, they should not be needed. The issues addressed in this 'cluster'—probationary periods, reviews and supervision—are designed to nip potentially serious problems in the bud. They also, and this is important for projects employing a lone worker, provide regular and structured opportunities to give the worker support and positive feedback. If properly planned and implemented, your monitoring and assessment procedures will have the capacity to contribute to both the personal development of your worker and the progress of the project's work.

Probationary periods
Your offer of employment may be dependent upon satisfactory completion of a probationary period, the length of which—between three and six months—will have been specified in the letter of appointment and written statement of terms and conditions. Its purpose is to allow time for you to assess the worker's suitability and performance in post and for the worker to decide whether he or she wishes to stay. During a probationary period, the minimum period of notice to be given on either side may be reduced. Take care not to extend a probationary period indefinitely—after one year of continuous employment the worker will be entitled to claim unfair dismissal.

Following the end of a probationary period, you have three options. It is likely, given the degree of care taken over the appointment process, that you will want to confirm the worker in post. At the end of the specified time, there may be aspects of the worker's performance—for example, poor time-keeping—with which you are unsatisfied. In these circumstances, you may decide to extend the period of probation for, say, another month. If there are more serious problems, such as repeated unauthorised absences, you may decide that the worker is not to be confirmed in post. This is not a decision to be undertaken lightly, so your reasons must be clear.

It is helpful, therefore, to decide in advance how you intend to monitor and assess your worker's performance during the probationary period. You should also make sure that the worker is made fully aware of the process, who is to be involved and the criteria by which performance will be assessed. Note that any criteria for assessment should always be based on the responsibilities set out in the job description: make sure, too, that any specific goals are appropriate to the length of the probationary period.

Above all, remember that the emphasis of a probationary period should be on the resolution, not the creation, of difficulties. In other words, as an employer, your first response to any problem should be to identify ways of supporting the worker to overcome it. If an extension to the probationary period is judged necessary, a programme of appropriate support should be provided.

In the majority of situations, where the worker is performing well and working relationships are good, the end of the probationary period passes by 'on the nod'. Whatever the degree of satisfaction with performance, it is always important to mark the end of the probationary period. This may happen via a formal review of progress, followed by a recommendation to the management committee to confirm the worker in post. Remember to communicate your decision: satisfied employers should be aware that their workers may not take this for granted. The act of confirmation not only removes an area of uncertainty, but may also boost confidence in the work.

Reviews
Even if your letter of appointment did not specify a probationary period, it is still a good idea to hold a review meeting. This meeting, unlike the probationary process, is not about deciding whether or not the worker is to be confirmed in post. It is an opportunity to discuss the job and how things are going.

This is especially important in situations where posts are new and/or workers are relatively isolated. The timing of the meeting should allow sufficient time for the worker to settle into the work, but also acknowledge the steep learning curve presented by any new job. Consequently, anything under three months is likely to be too short to be useful, but a year is probably too long to wait. You might, if the worker is isolated, consider conducting the review at the end of the first six months.

You may, at a later stage, decide to hold a regular annual review, which is sometimes referred to as an appraisal. In some large organisations, although the emphasis of a properly implemented and fair scheme should be on development, appraisals may be linked to grading and pay levels. The word 'appraisal' may therefore be regarded with suspicion by some workers. Moreover, if you are not in a position to offer either promotion or pay increases, you may risk creating expectations which cannot be fulfilled. It may be better to use the more modest term 'review', which is less threatening whilst not excluding the possibility of challenge. To create the trust and honesty essential to the process, the purpose of a review must be clearly defined and communicated to all involved.

The purpose of an annual review is to enable a 'long view' and to address the big issues which cannot easily be tackled in supervision, such as the overall development of the project.

It may help the process if the review takes place 'off-site': one city-based worker and the management committee representative responsible for conducting her review used to combine the process with lunch in a country pub. The worker reports, 'Getting away from the project was really important—it helped me to put problems into perspective and for once I had someone's undivided attention.'

Although a relaxed atmosphere is important, a review is more than a chat. In order to be of benefit to all parties, reviews should be carefully structured. A possible format for the review, devised by a group of church-related community workers in the north-west, is provided in Box I. Note that the emphasis of the questions is on development rather than judgement. Their purpose is to enable an overview of the work (which includes both the assessment of past achievements and the agreement of future objectives); to address issues of support; and to identify development needs (which may be met either by training or work experience). The reviewer should take responsibility for recording key points and any agreements reached on priorities, support and training needs. The summary could be signed by both the reviewer and the worker and used as the basis for next year's review.

Box I: Questions for an annual review

Looking at your job description, say in which key tasks you have done well during the past year? Give examples.

Which key tasks in your job description have not gone well? Give examples.

Are there any inappropriate key tasks in your job description? Or any that have been omitted? Please specify them.

How do you describe your overall performance in the past year? Summarise in one or two sentences.

List targets relating to your key tasks that you intend to achieve in the next year. (A target is a measurable objective which can be achieved in a specific time.)

List what you see to be your specific training and/or experience needs during the coming year.

Describe any particular help or support you feel you need in achieving your targets.

source: Network North West/The William Temple Foundation

Supervision

If the purpose of a review is to enable both project and worker to take a long-term view of the work, the purpose of supervision is to provide an opportunity for workers to discuss their work on a more regular basis (ideally every four to six weeks). Some projects, especially single worker projects, prefer to contract supervision to an external consultant, but this is not essential. Unless the post requires specialist expertise, a well-prepared line manager or management committee member is perfectly able to undertake responsibility for supervision. You will find a simple format for a supervision session in Box J. In order to obtain maximum benefit, the purpose of the sessions and the responsibilities of both participants should be clarified.

Supervision is more than a friendly chat or an excuse for a whinge on either side. The aim is to provide a structured opportunity to evaluate short and medium term progress against a work plan; to deal with problems; and to set priorities and control workloads. You can help by ensuring that sessions are a regular, firm commitment; by preparing for sessions (and expecting your worker to come prepared); by checking that agreements made on both sides are carried out; by keeping notes as a basis for subsequent sessions.

Please note that, although commitment and cooperation will be required from both participants, it is your responsibility to model the professionalism required from your worker.

Second, although support is an important dimension of the supervision process, be careful that sessions are not entirely dominated by the worker's personal needs. The manager of a mother-and-toddler project reports on her first experience of giving supervision: 'because we were a women's project, I tried to be understanding about domestic problems affecting the worker, but eventually that was all we ever talked about—so real problem areas in performance were not addressed.' Good supervision also aims to establish the accountability of the worker to both the project and its users: your responsibilities as an employer extend beyond pastoral care for an individual.

Thirdly, beware of going to the opposite extreme. It is easy, especially for inexperienced or insecure supervisors, to make the mistake of being too heavy-handed. A responsible supervisor may occasionally need to challenge or stretch a worker. However, the overall emphasis of supervision should be on creative problem-solving and development. Please note that it is not acceptable to treat supervision as an extension of your project's disciplinary procedure: concerns voiced in supervision do not constitute verbal warnings.

> **Box J: Questions for a supervision session**
>
> This simple structure is designed to address the different objectives of a supervision session—obtaining an overview of progress; evaluating the work; identifying support needs; and setting priorities for the next stage. For maximum benefit the questions, which may be adapted to suit particular circumstances, should be considered by supervisor and worker beforehand.
>
> **Overview**
> What has been done since the last session? How have these achievements contributed to the direction and progress of the work plan?
>
> **Evaluation**
> What has gone well? Why? How can the worker build on success? What has not gone well? Why? How can specific problems be addressed? How can work be improved?
>
> **Support**
> Are particular people or groups posing a problem? Are other situations affecting the work? Is additional training and/or support required?
>
> **Priorities**
> Is the workload realistic? What should be the priorities for the next session? What needs to be done before the next supervision? By the worker? By the supervisor?

3.5 Support and development

Having striven to fulfil your obligations, you may be relieved to discover that none of the issues discussed in this final cluster is a legal requirement. But, given the considerable investment in appointing a worker, to neglect responsibility for further support and development would be counterproductive. Attention to the issues discussed below—induction programmes, support and training—is not compulsory, but may make all the difference to the relationship with your worker and the smooth progress of the work.

Induction programmes

A worker with experience of running a series of job-creation schemes comments, 'I can't face walking into another empty church hall and having, as a first job, to find myself a desk and chair.'

Her experience is perhaps an extreme version of that faced by many workers entering a new job, in which the most basic information, contacts and resources are not provided. If well-planned, even the simplest induction programme will help you to avoid these pitfalls. Its purpose is to ensure that the worker gets to know the project, their role within it and any other organisations in the area doing related work. Since the main focus is on learning, although they do overlap, an induction programme is separate from a probationary period.

Local circumstances are likely to vary to such an extent that a set induction format is not helpful. You should aim to include at least the following five dimensions in your induction programme (which could be allocated to different members of the management committee). Try, in each area, to find an appropriate balance between basic support and sufficient space for workers to find their own feet. For example, although it is a good idea to timetable initial meetings with key people and groups, workers still need time to absorb information and the scope to exercise their own initiative.

- **Place**
  The immediate priority is the workplace. From day one, workers need to be familiar with the building—location of toilets, fire exits, kitchen, telephones, office, filing system etc—and rules governing its use, for example, health and safety and security procedures. Make sure, even if the project has no other paid staff, that workers are introduced to other users of the premises. Remember to allow some quiet time for settling into new surroundings and becoming familiar with any other information provided
- **Information**
  Needs are likely to include basic reference works (telephone book, local *A to Z*, diocesan or CVS handbook); information about the area (community

profiles or statistics); information about the project (history, structures and minutes of the relevant management committee); and lists of key contacts. If your project is well-established, you will have files to be handed on. Please note that dumping boxes on a desk is rarely helpful.

- **People**
  Arrange for a few key people to be around on the first day, but beware of overload. In the first fortnight, timetable a series of meetings with a wider group of people associated with the project: users, volunteers, management committee members and any other local people involved in the work. These will not only provide useful personal introductions, but also enable the worker to learn gradually about the different dimensions of the project.

- **Liaisons**
  You will need to ensure that your worker has a list of agencies and organisations (statutory and voluntary) with which they are likely to be involved. If there are any scheduled meetings at which their presence is expected, make sure that dates and venues are provided.

- **Work**
  New workers are usually keen to get involved as soon as possible, so your programme should provide opportunities for the worker and line manager to discuss the job. It is a good idea for the line manager to identify a few specific, short-term tasks which the worker can begin immediately. Remember also to allow scope for sharing ideas for medium-to-long-term development and the role of the worker in moving the project forward.

Support

Support has already been mentioned in the context of supervision. But, whereas the main focus of supervision should be on the work, the main focus of support is on the worker. Some workers may find that regular supervision sessions are sufficient to meet their needs, but there may be situations in which additional support is needed.

The suggestion may come from the worker: an example would be a single worker project in which there is no opportunity for informal support from co-workers. It might also come from the employer: an example might be a situation, such as the mother-and-toddler project, in which personal issues hinder the development of the work. Here a separate support structure might enable appropriate boundaries to be established and observed. Bear in mind that such structures need not be permanent: they may also be made available on a temporary basis during a time of personal crisis, say, a major bereavement affecting the worker.

Support structures can be very informal—for example, a designated person who is easily and regularly available to the worker. Alternatively, a regular support group might be formed. Ideally, although the initial suggestion might come from the employer, the identification of the most appropriate support person and/or the formation and running of the support group should be done in collaboration with the worker.

There is just one caveat: it is best if people with responsibility for managing the worker are not involved in a support role. It is, sadly, not unknown for managers to abuse confidences shared in support groups, or for workers to use such groups as a means of subtly manipulating or disabling management. In order to avoid a potential conflict of interests, management and support roles should be kept separate.

Training

However limited your budget, you should aim to include money for training. There is an obvious benefit to the worker in terms of opportunities for personal development—especially important if a contract is offered on a fixed-term basis and the worker needs to acquire or develop marketable skills. Meanwhile, from the project's perspective, training is both a constructive response to problems identified in supervision or reviews and an investment in one of its most important resources: projects which are happy to update a computer system may be unwilling to spend a fraction of the same money on updating a worker's skills. It could be argued that, if contracts are fixed-term, such investment is wasted. But projects gain from the increased motivation and loyalty of valued workers. From a long-term perspective, your investment in the resource of a trained worker can be seen as a lasting contribution from the project to the church and the wider community.

Training can be addressed in a variety of ways. For example, if practical experience in a particular area of work is missing, 'on the job' training could be offered. An example would be a worker who has identified in supervision a need to gain experience in working with a particular group, say, Asian elders. This could be addressed via planned experience with that group within the regular work programme. If appropriate opportunities cannot be provided in-house, they might be negotiated externally. By shadowing a worker in a relevant project, the necessary experience may be acquired.

In-house training opportunities specifically designed to meet the needs of your project may also be offered. These are more appropriate to situations in which there is a group rather than an individual need. You might prefer to use in-house training in situations where a new development has implications for the project as a whole, rather than just for the worker. Examples would be workshops on issues such as personal security or the use of a new email system, which will also be relevant to the needs of project users, volunteers and management committee members.

External opportunities are useful in situations where specialist expertise, not available within the project, is needed. These can be short-term or long-term depending on circumstances and need. For example, an employer might fund attendance at workshops on specific topics such as fundraising or child protection: your local CVS is a good source of information on relevant training opportunities, as is the Directory of Social Change*. Alternatively, you may wish to support your worker through a course of extended study towards a recognised qualification, such as a diploma in youth and community work, either via day release or a distance learning course.

Once you have identified a training need, you should consider all the available options and their appropriateness to your circumstances and budget. As you do so, you should take two other factors into account: the varying cost implications of different forms of training (both money and time) and the principle of equal opportunities. These factors may interact: one worker is restricted to 'on the job' training whilst another is funded on a prestigious course with an external training provider. In order to ensure good practice, even if you have just one full-time worker, you are recommended to draw up a training policy for your project: remember that any volunteers, casual and part-time staff will also have training needs.

Checklist

✔ Taking a realistic view of available resources and expertise, can the payroll be handled within the project? If not, what alternatives are available to you? Who is responsible for researching them?

✔ Did your original budget include any provision for pension contributions? If not, what can be done to remedy the omission as soon as possible?

✔ Have you considered your responsibilities in the event of sickness or pregnancy? Is basic information available for reference should the need arise?

✔ Has a risk assessment been undertaken for your project? If not, who should be responsible?

✔ Is a general health and safety policy a legal requirement for your project? Are specific policies also required? If you already have general or specific policies, are you confident that you can deliver everything you say you will?

✔ Have you checked whether your current level of insurance cover is sufficient to meet your new responsibilities?

✔ If you have not already drawn up disciplinary and grievance procedures, have you set a deadline by which they are to be produced? Have you decided who is to be involved at each stage?
If you have specified a probationary period, how is this to be handled? How will the new worker be kept informed of the process and outcomes of the probationary period?

✔ Has the designated line manager any experience of giving supervision? If not, what resources are available to help with preparation? (You will find relevant reading in Appendix A and can obtain advice on appropriate training via your CVS).

✔ If you intend to introduce an annual review, how can this be planned to benefit both project and worker?

✔ What action is needed under each of the five dimensions of an induction programme? Before the worker takes up post? And afterwards?

✔ What support for training can your project currently offer? What do you think should be included in your training policy?

4 Reviewing

When you are celebrating success in obtaining the money to employ a worker, you are probably reluctant to think about when the money runs out. Don't be. You need to think about the outcomes of the work and the options for the future in order to plan the employment relationship well. This guide emphasises the importance of taking a long-term view.

In this final section, you are invited to imagine that you are entering the last year of funding. What are the issues that confront you? What are the available options for the project? What are their implications for your responsibilities as an employer? This section aims to provide a starting point for tackling the issues, namely an evaluation of the work undertaken during the funding period. It is followed by a discussion of the employment implications of three options—drawing the work to a close, continuing the work and redeveloping the work. In the checklist, you are invited to use the long-term view as a basis for reviewing any decisions about the employment relationship that you have made so far.

4.1 Evaluating the work

In the previous section you considered various structures for monitoring and assessment—probationary periods, reviews and supervision—all of which were primarily concerned with the performance of the worker. It is important to emphasise that the important issue in evaluation is not the performance or prospects of the worker. It is the work done by the project during the funding period. The findings of an evaluation process certainly have implications for the employment relationship, but decisions about whether or not to continue the worker in employment should not be included.

Evaluation of a project's work should not take place as a knee-jerk response to a crisis. To be of real value, it should be planned well in advance and the objectives must be clearly defined, agreed and communicated to all involved.

If you are not deciding the future of the worker, what is the purpose of an evaluation? Evaluation is often undertaken because of a requirement to report to a funding body. It establishes the accountability of the project to the organisations providing financial support for the work, so enabling them to make best use of funds. As well as satisfying the requirements of their funding bodies, projects may gain additional benefits from the exercise. It can enable them to improve their effectiveness in meeting existing needs; to prioritise investment of their limited resources; and to identify new needs. Even if you are not required to conduct an evaluation for an external organisation, you are strongly advised to do so for the benefit of your project and to set up self-evaluation practices.

When, and how often, should an evaluation be conducted? If the purpose is to satisfy an existing funding body, or to present a strong case for supporting an established project to a potential funder, you should aim to conduct your evaluation at the beginning of the final year of the funding period. The exercise should be completed *at least* six months before funds run out. Even if you are not under the same pressure to deliver, you should aim to evaluate your work every three years. This is because the context in which you operate can change dramatically within this period, which may have major implications for your project. For example, a change in social policy which puts pressure on lone parents to obtain paid employment might mean that a family advice centre has to develop to meet new needs.

An important issue to consider is what kind of information you need to gather. If you are accounting to an external body, the type of information may already be laid down: keeping records of 'numbers helped into work' is a common requirement for a job club in receipt of public funds. Even if you are not required to meet the predefined criteria of an external agency, you should still record and analyse any measurable achievements. Examples might be the number of users of your service, or events organised.

It is also important to think about how you intend to collect and record 'soft data' such as comments on feedback forms or interviews with project users. This material puts flesh on dry bones: systematically collected and carefully handled, soft data is valuable. Statistics complemented by soft data can create a more interesting and varied report—the power of 'readability' should not be underestimated.

Do not forget, too, to put evaluation of the project within a broader social context: showing its contribution to the life of the community testifies to the value of your work.

An issue to consider at a later stage is who should undertake the evaluation: someone from within the project or an outsider experienced in conducting evaluations? Both external and internal evaluators have advantages and disadvantages. An outsider is able to see the project through new eyes; may therefore find it easier to provide an objective assessment; and will not usually stand to gain from the process. However, an outsider may not fully understand the situation and the people and may be perceived as threatening by those involved. By contrast an internal evaluator will have a greater understanding, but may in consequence find it hard to be objective. There is also a risk that an internal evaluator may use the process to serve their own interests or promote a personal 'line' on the project's future. It is important to be clear about what you want to achieve before deciding what is best for your project – external evaluation, internal evaluation, or even a combination of both?

You will find more detailed advice on the principles and practice of evaluation from the specialist organisation, Charities Evaluation Services*, or in many of the general publications listed in Appendix A. One of them, Sandy Adirondack's comprehensive guide, *Just About Managing*, proposes four general criteria for successful evaluation which underline two of the points already made. First, an evaluation should have clear, written objectives: you need to be clear about the purpose of the evaluation and precisely what you aim to achieve. Second, your evaluation needs to be based on solid information. It is important, therefore, to establish systems for collecting data about your project from the outset. The third criterion is willingness to be self-critical. An ability to identify weaknesses and strategies for improvement is more likely to receive serious attention than an empty public relations exercise. Finally, if evaluation is to be of practical use, a project must be willing to use its findings as a basis for change.

Please note that, to increase the chances of the evaluation being both useful and used, it should be concise, clear and jargon free.

Once you have completed your report, you are in a position to consider the available options for the future of your project. The findings may support a strong case for seeking continuation funding: the project may be the only or even the most successful provider of your particular service within the neighbourhood. Alternatively, you may find that your success consists of making the need you set out to address redundant, in which case you might consider either developing a new area of work or closing down the project altogether. It is important to be aware that each option has different implications for the employment relationship. As you address the issues, you need to strike an appropriate balance between the fulfilment of your responsibilities and recognition that decisions about the future also involve factors other than safeguarding a particular job or worker.

4.2 Concluding the work

Probably the least popular option for any management committee is to close the project altogether. This may happen because the resources—human as well as financial—are no longer available to support continuation of the work. To decide on this option does not necessarily imply failure: a project may cease to operate because it has successfully achieved its goals. To become redundant for these reasons is, from the perspective of the project, a major cause for celebration. But closure of a project, for whatever reason, inevitably results in redundancy for the worker. If this outcome is a possibility for your project, it is important to clarify the nature of redundancy, your responsibilities in the process and the procedures to be followed.

Redundancy is a way of ensuring that a contract of employment can be fairly terminated. Genuine redundancy only applies in the following circumstances: if the workplace moves significantly or disappears; if an organisation is closing and all the jobs are disappearing; if an individual's job disappears because of reorganisation. In the case of a decision to close a project, the second circumstance is assumed. If on the basis of your evaluation you decide to develop the project in a new direction, the third circumstance might be the reason for redundancy. In this situation, you need to be sure that the redundancy is genuine: if you make your worker redundant, and the job they undertook still exists, the redundant worker could bring a case to an Employment Tribunal.

A related issue when considering redundancy is the nature of the contract issued. If you issued a permanent contract, the situation is clear and the redundancy procedures relatively straightforward. If you issued a fixed-term contract, the situation is rather more complicated. Workers employed on fixed-term contracts have the same rights as workers on permanent contracts, but, until very recently, employers were often advised to include a 'waiver clause' which protected them against claims for redundancy pay or unfair dismissal if a fixed-term contract was not renewed. It is still possible in a fixed-term contract of two or more years to include a clause protecting the employer against claims for redundancy pay. However, under the Employment Relations Bill (1999), the right to claim unfair dismissal can no longer be waived. The employment implications of this ruling have yet to be clarified, so employers should take legal advice if there is any doubt about how to proceed when a fixed-term contract is due for expiry or renewal.

Having clarified the nature of redundancy, what are your responsibilities as an employer? Not surprisingly, especially in church and community-based organisations with strong, people-centred values, redundancy is a course of action that many management committees are reluctant to take. Consequently, the process is often handled badly. A worker describes her experience in a project with severe financial difficulties, 'The personal implications were clear, but the management committee at first wouldn't acknowledge the problem and then acted as if the inevitable was a big surprise.'

If you are facing a situation likely to result in redundancy for your worker, you must assume full responsibility for any decisions made. To put your head in the sand or to deny responsibility is not good practice. It may feel uncomfortable (and workers may do their best to reinforce discomfort), but this is no excuse for ignoring and/or declining responsibility for the situation.

Another issue to consider in the event of redundancy is your own role within the process. It is likely that, far from washing your hands of the situation, you will want to be as supportive as you can towards your worker. You need to ensure that the support you offer is appropriate to your role as an employer: redundancy is one of those occasions when you need to take special care to ensure that proper roles and relationships are observed. The redundant worker quoted above found that, 'the first response of the chair of my management committee, a minister, was to offer me counselling, but what I really needed to know was where I stood.'

Support does not translate as tea and sympathy. It means managing the process professionally and fairly, ensuring that correct procedures are followed and responsibilities fulfilled.

The procedures to be followed by employers needing to make staff redundant vary according to the size of the organisation and the number of workers affected. General guidance on the main issues is given below. Remember that these are subject to change. If you have to make a worker redundant, you must seek advice at the earliest possible opportunity. If you do not, and fail to handle the situation according to the correct procedures, you may be liable to a claim for unfair dismissal. Since, with effect from 25 October 1999, the ceiling for compensation has risen from £12,000 to £50,000, neglect may prove costly.

Selection
In the case of closure, selection for redundancy does not apply. In other circumstances, projects employing more than one worker need to ensure that selection for redundancy is fair. It is automatically unfair if selection takes place on the grounds of pregnancy or maternity; health and safety; assertion of a statutory right; union membership; or on the basis of race or gender.

Employers also need to set clear selection criteria and ensure that these are communicated and applied across the board. These may be consist of non-compulsory criteria (such as voluntary redundancy or early retirement), or compulsory criteria (such as proficiency through skills and qualifications, length of service, or attendance records).

Consultation
In a small project employing a single worker, you are not obliged either to notify the authorities or to consult with trade unions. However, if your worker is a member of a union recognised by the employer, you should at least aim to inform the relevant union representative. More importantly, you should be aware that case law has shown that, for a redundancy dismissal to be fair, an individual who is to be made redundant should always be consulted.

What does consultation mean in practice? In organisations with a number of staff, if a job disappears, consultation is often used as a way of seeking alternative solutions such as redeployment. If a single worker project closes, such options are not available. In fact, the only situation in which redeployment may be relevant is one in which redevelopment of the work results in an entirely new job being created. The issues to be addressed in these circumstances are discussed in the relevant section below. Even in situations where options are very limited, consultation need not be an empty exercise. It still has the benefit of keeping workers informed of the decision, the likely timetable for redundancy and their rights in the process. Decisions should be communicated and confirmed by letter.

Notice periods
Under the Employment Rights Act (1996), employees must be given notice of redundancy. The minimum length of notice is one week after one month's and up to two years' service, and one week for each continuous year of employment after two years' service up to a maximum of twelve weeks. If a longer period is given in the contract of employment, the contractual notice period has priority. It is, according to NCVO, good practice for all employees to receive at least one month's notice of redundancy. If workers have two years of continuous service, they also have a legal entitlement to a written statement setting out the reasons for the termination of their employment. It is good practice to do this in all cases.

The only exception to the above is when a worker is employed on a fixed-term contract, either because funding is available for a set number of years, or because a particular job is to be completed within a specified period. In such situations there is no need to give notice because, at the end of the fixed term, the employment is at an end. It is still important to include within the contract of employment a notice period which enables either the employer or the employee to terminate the contract before the fixed-term has expired. If you do not do this, and your funding collapses half way through, you will find that you are obliged to employ the worker for the duration of the contract.

Redundancy payments
If you are unable to offer another suitable job, your worker becomes entitled to a redundancy payment. This applies not only to all workers on permanent or open contracts, but also to fixed-term workers. The only category of employee with no entitlement to redundancy pay is a fixed-term worker who has specifically waived the right to claim. Redundancy payment should be allowed for in calculating budgets. You will find more information on statutory requirements in Box K. More detailed information, including calculation tables, is available in the Department of Trade and Industry information leaflet *Redundancy Payments* (PL808). Note that this relates to the statutory minimum: employers may choose to offer better terms.

Paid time off
Every employee given notice of redundancy should be given reasonable paid time off during the notice period to look for another job. There is no legal definition of 'reasonable', but it is considered to be good practice to allow as much time as the person needs. This would cover time for obvious job-hunting activities, such as filling out application forms, preparing for, and attending, job interviews. Time for making arrangements for training for future employment is also included. Further information is available in the Department of Trade and Industry information leaflet, *Facing Redundancy? Time off for job hunting or to arrange training* (PL703).

Support
The fulfilment of responsibilities does not preclude an employer from offering additional support to a redundant worker during a stressful period. If so, as with support groups, you should try to ensure that boundaries are observed. For example, although it would be inappropriate for employers to counsel a worker made redundant by their decision, they might wish to refer a staff member to a person outside the management structures. Alternatively, an employer might fund a session with a career consultant. If you wish to offer extra support, check its appropriateness with your worker.

References
Employers have no obligation to give a reference. But if the project is closing, and the worker is without another job, it is a good idea to ensure that the relevant records of the worker's employment with the project are kept for future reference. It may be useful to write a standard reference to be kept on file.

Box K: Redundancy payments

What is a redundancy payment?
Redundancy payments are designed to compensate employees for the loss of their job.

Who can claim a redundancy payment?
All employees have a right to redundancy pay if they have worked for an employer continuously for two years and are below the normal retirement age. Thus employees aged under 18 and 65 or over are not entitled to redundancy payments and an employee aged 64 loses one-twelfth of redundancy payment for each month over 64.

How is the payment calculated?
The statutory level of payment is based on the number of complete years of service and the age of the employee:

- half a week's pay for each complete year over the age of 18 and under the age of 22
- one week's pay for each complete year aged 22 or more but less than age 41
- one and a half week's pay for each complete year aged 41 or more
- a week's pay is either the actual amount received each week or £220, whichever is lower.
- an employee can be compensated for a maximum of 20 years.

The employer must give the redundant employee a written statement detailing the payment and how it has been calculated.

Who is responsible for the payment?
Until 1989, employers could claim the cost of redundancy pay from the State. However, they are now responsible for making the payment from their own funds and this should be built into budgets.

Policy

It may seem early in the day to be considering a redundancy policy, especially if only one worker is involved. However, as with your disciplinary and grievance procedures, it is better to address the issues before the event. Moreover, if the result of evaluation is not closure but expansion of the project, you may find yourself in the situation of taking on more workers.

A good redundancy policy, setting out both process and provisions, would enable you to take decisions without bias or prejudice against particular individuals. Remember to keep the budgetary implications of your policy under constant review: do you need to set up a contingency fund to enable you to meet your statutory and/or contractual obligations towards your workers?

4.3 Continuing the work

A more popular option for projects, especially those aiming to provide a core service, is to embark upon a search for continuation funding. The challenges involved in seeking continuation funding for what is, essentially, the same work should not be underestimated. However, as suggested at the beginning of this guide, the task is not impossible if you can demonstrate some or all of the following criteria: continuing (or even increased) need for your service; consistent success in meeting (or exceeding) targets; and willingness to constantly make improvements and innovations in the service you offer.

If your bid proves successful, your next task is to address the implications for the worker. Once again, although the differences are no longer so marked, these vary according to the nature of the contract originally issued.

Fundraising

Detailed advice on fundraising is beyond the scope of this guide. However, if you think that this is a likely option for your project, be sure to begin your search in good time.

An experienced fundraiser comments, 'every autumn I get calls from projects worried because their funding runs out at Christmas and I have to tell them that they've missed the boat.'

The absolute minimum period to allow for fundraising is six months and it is probably more realistic to allow a full year. It is a good idea, from the outset, for someone on the management committee to monitor and collect information on likely sources, in particular any new initiatives which may be helpful for your project. This will give your search a head start and help you to develop the most appropriate 'spin' for your next funding bid.

Fundraising is a time-consuming activity. A worker for a project set up to meet the needs of child refugees speaks of her experience, 'searching for financial support accounts for more than 25 per cent of staff time—and that's time lost to the children and the job.'

The time factor therefore has implications for decisions about who should assume responsibility for fundraising: a member of the management committee or the project worker? In order to allow workers to get on with the jobs they were appointed to do, fundraising should be allocated to someone without day-to-day responsibility for running the project. However, people who serve on management committees (often in a voluntary capacity) do not always have the time to devote to the work. In many projects much of the fundraising is likely to be undertaken by the worker. If this is the situation facing your project, one strategy is to form a fundraising working group in order to research the options, develop strategies and apportion the workload according to the skills of the group members.

Finally, remember that expert help is at hand. You may have access to advice within the structures of your own denomination, for example, through a diocesan Church Urban Fund officer. If not, and even if you do, it is always a good idea to contact your local CVS. It may offer some or all of the following: specialist training programmes; a library with printed and electronic sources of information; and the services of an adviser who can offer help with applications as well as guidance on the most likely sources. You may also wish to contact the Directory of Social Change*, which has a proven track record as a provider of quality training programme and publications. The current catalogue includes handbooks on how to prepare applications and a series of comprehensive guides (to company giving; to major and local trusts; to specialist funding; to funding from government departments and agencies; to European funding; and to the National Lottery). Other national sources include NCVO* (especially good on popular, accessible guides to fundraising within 'the Brussels maze'); the Charities Aid Foundation*; and the fundraising helpline run by the Charity Commission* (020 7210 4630).

Contract renewal

If you succeed in obtaining continuation funding, the probability is that your existing worker will continue in post. In fact, if the worker has been continuously employed by the project for more than one year, a decision not to continue the worker in post would be very risky indeed. Under the Employment Rights Act (1996), employers must consider offering a worker threatened with redundancy another post, if one exists. To make your worker redundant and then to advertise another post with similar duties and responsibilities would lay the project open to a charge of unfair dismissal.

Dissatisfaction with performance is unlikely to be accepted by an Employment Tribunal as a reason for not continuing the worker in post. If poor performance is an issue, you need to tackle the problem directly via the disciplinary procedure. It is never acceptable to use a new funding period as an excuse for dismissing a worker.

If the existing worker is employed on a permanent or open contract, there is no need for the worker's contract to be renewed. You should, however, be aware that continuing the same worker in post has financial implications: if you appointed the worker on an incremental scale, salary costs will rise until the worker reaches the top point of the band. Those rights acquired through length of service, such as entitlement to redundancy pay, will also increase. You therefore need to ensure that your budget is able to meet these accumulating responsibilities. They are, after all, a small price to pay for the continuing asset of an experienced worker whose commitment to your work has been tried and tested.

A more likely situation, given current funding regimes, is that the project worker was originally employed on a fixed-term contract. Until very recently, contract renewal was an uncertain area for fixed-term workers, since employers could require the worker to waive the right to claim for unfair dismissal. This practice is now illegal and compensation levels for successful claims are higher. At the time of writing, the implications of this change in legislation are unclear, but one consequence is that the situation of the fixed-term worker is now much closer to that of the permanent worker. If the same job remains to be done, you should aim to confirm the existing worker in post. The main difference is that a new contract has to be issued.

What are the issues to consider when issuing a new contract? It is important, first of all, to observe good practice: workers should not be employed on a series of fixed-term contracts because of concerns about future funding or because of a desire to avoid liability for redundancy pay. If you are continuing the worker in the same post, consider offering a permanent or open contract. Second, if you do decide in favour of a fixed-term contract, you need to make sure that the first contract is renewed and not just allowed to run on: to do this would mean that the worker is then regarded as being in permanent employment, with full redundancy rights. Third, remember that your worker's continuity of service dates from the date of the original contract and not the date upon which the contract was renewed. Finally, although you could include a waiver clause within the new contract to avoid liability for redundancy pay, this is a very uncertain area of the law. To avoid potentially costly mistakes, you should seek legal advice.

4.4 Redeveloping the work

A third option suggested by your evaluation might be a complete rethink of the focus and direction of your project's work. For example, a project set up to provide after-school play activities on church premises might discover that the real need was for a homework club in partnership with the local school. Its management committee might then decide to use the end of a funding period as an opportunity to redevelop the project to meet emerging needs.

The main advantage of redevelopment is that funding opportunities are likely to increase: generally speaking, it is much easier for projects to obtain money for innovation than continuation funds.

This fact of life is also viewed as a major disadvantage. The chair of an established church-based community project, one of the first to receive support from the National Lottery Charities Board, speaks for many less successful projects, 'Why do we have to keep reinventing ourselves—isn't it enough to keep doing what we know we can do well?'

Who cannot think of a project that 'used to do good work', but has since 'lost its way' in the competition for funds? For this reason many management committees criticise change that appears to be too funding-led. However, if you are continually reviewing the quality and relevance of the service you offer, this criticism need not hold. It is important to remember that the fourth criterion for successful evaluation identified by Sandy Adirondack is willingness to change.

One consequence of redeveloping a project's work is that the current job description will have to be reviewed. It may be useful at this point for the management committee to repeat the exercise of drawing up a new job description in consultation with the worker. Do not forget that any amendments to a job description must be mutually agreed.

If the reworked job description includes significantly increased responsibilities—such as the management of other workers or increased budgets—this should be reflected in the grading and pay levels. You should also check that the worker's skills and experience are appropriate to the demands of the new job description: is additional training necessary and how can it be provided? If the management committee has attended to training needs and opportunities throughout the worker's employment, this may not be needed.

It may be tempting, especially if a fixed-term contract is due to expire, simply to advertise a new job on the open market. If so, the first thing to consider is whether or not the existing worker's job has effectively disappeared as a result of the reorganisation of the project. Unless a case of genuine redundancy applies, regardless of the nature of the contract, this would constitute unfair dismissal.

Even if the case for redundancy is genuine, the law encourages employers to offer alternative employment. Generally speaking, a job is considered to be suitable if it is on a similar rate of pay; has a similar status; is within the employee's capability; and does not involve unreasonable inconvenience such as a major alteration to travel-to-work time or working hours. Even if these general criteria are not met, an employee is still free to accept an offer of alternative employment.

If such an offer is accepted, an otherwise redundant worker is entitled to a statutory four-week trial period in the new job. If employment is terminated by either party during the trial period, the employee will be treated as redundant and any right to redundancy pay preserved. The only exception is where an employee has terminated employment unreasonably.

It may be that, despite everyone's best efforts, the existing worker is not suited to the new job. To make a worker redundant in such circumstances is never easy. However, just as closure does not mean that a project has failed, redundancy does not mean that the employer has failed. If the redundancy is clearly genuine, if you have done everything you can to explore alternative solutions and if you have fulfilled your responsibilities to your worker, as an employer you have succeeded. Moreover, if you have consistently managed the employment relationship in such a way that your worker has had opportunity to learn and develop, he or she is returning to the labour market with increased skills and experience and greater 'employability'. This benefits the worker and also the organisations and communities with whom the worker becomes involved. This gift alone testifies to the power of good practice to make a difference beyond the life of a project.

Checklist

The following questions are designed to encourage you to double-check decisions and to help you to prepare and answer for the inevitable question, 'what next?'

✔ What do you expect to happen when your period of funding ends? To your project? To your worker?

✔ What kind of information do you need to collect in order to monitor and assess your work? What systems might you put in place at the beginning?

✔ Are your recruitment procedures (advertisement and job description) sufficiently informative about how, and for how long, the post is funded?

✔ Does your job description make provision for mutually agreed amendments?

✔ Does the contract state clearly if the contract is fixed-term and, if so, include an expiry date? Are normal notice periods also included? Should the contract include a 'waiver clause'?

✔ Do you have a written redundancy policy? If not, who should be responsible for writing one?

✔ Does your budget allow you to fulfil your responsibilities in the event of redundancy? Do you need a contingency fund?

✔ If you hope to continue your work beyond the current funding period, how do you plan to monitor and research new funding opportunities? What resources and assistance are available locally?

Appendix A: Useful resources

These are some of the most accessible and affordable guides to employment law and practice currently available. The majority are written with the needs of small, voluntary organisations in mind. The church-related texts referred to in the main text are listed separately, together with contact information.

General

Sandy ADIRONDACK, *Just About Managing*, third edition (London, London Voluntary Service Council, 1998)

Sandy ADIRONDACK and James Sinclair TAYLOR, *The Voluntary Sector Legal Handbook* (London, Directory of Social Change 1996)

ADVISORY, CONCILIATION AND ARBITRATION SERVICE, *Discipline at Work. The ACAS Advisory Handbook* (London, ACAS, February 1999)

COMMISSION FOR RACIAL EQUALITY, *Race Relations Code of Practice. For the Elimination of Racial Discrimination and the Promotion of Equality of Opportunity in Employment* (London, Commission for Racial Equality, 1984)

EQUAL OPPORTUNITIES COMMISSION, *Code of Practice on Sex Discrimination. Equal Opportunities Policies, Procedures and Practices in Employment* (Manchester, Equal Opportunities Commission, no date)

EQUAL OPPORTUNITIES COMMISSION, *Guidelines for Equal Opportunities Employers* (Manchester, Equal Opportunities Commission, 1986)

Marie-Therese FEUERSTEIN, *Partners in Evaluation. Evaluating Development and Community Programmes with Participants* (London, Macmillan, 1986)

Duncan FORBES, Ruth HAYES and Jacki REASON, *Voluntary but not Amateur*, fifth edition (London, London Voluntary Service Council, 1998)

Sarah HARGREAVES, Christina MORTON and Gill TAYLOR, *Managing Absence: A Handbook for Managers in Public and Voluntary Organisations* (London, Russell House Publishing Ltd, 1998)

Al HINDE and Charlie KAVANAGH, *The Health and Safety Handbook*, edited by Jill Barlow (London, Directory of Social Change in association with Liverpool Occupational Health Project, 1998)

Ian HUNTER, *The Which? Guide to Employment. Rights and Tactics in the Workplace* (London, Which? Books, 1998)

LABOUR RESEARCH DEPARTMENT, *The Law at Work* (London, LRD Publications, 1998)

Alan LAWRIE, *The Complete Guide to Creating and Managing New Projects* (London, Directory of Social Change supported by Nat West, 1996)

Elizabeth POTTER and David SMELLIE, *Managing Staff Problems Fairly: A Guide for Voluntary Organisations* (Kingston-upon-Thames, Croner Publications, 1996)

NATIONAL ASSOCIATION OF COUNCILS FOR VOLUNTARY SERVICE, *The Employment Handbook*, second edition, (Sheffield, NACVS, 1999)

NATIONAL COUNCIL FOR VOLUNTARY ORGANISATION, *The Good Employment Guide for the Voluntary Sector*, second edition, (London, NCVO, 1999)

Kate SAYER, *A Practical Guide to PAYE for Charities* (London, Directory of Social Change in association with Sayer Vincent Chartered Accountants, 1995)

Gill TAYLOR, *Managing Recruitment and Selection* (London, Directory of Social Change, 1996)

Gill TAYLOR, *Managing Conflict* (London, Directory of Social Change, 1999)

Gill TAYLOR and Christine THORNTON, *Managing People* (London, Directory of Social Change, 1995)

Church-related

BISHOPS' COMMITTEE FOR ADULT CHRISTIAN EDUCATION, Magenta Pack. *Looseleaf collection of resources and information relating to the employment of lay people in pastoral work in Catholic Church settings* (Enquiries to the Pastoral Formation Office, 152 Brownlow Hill, Liverpool L3 5RQ)

DIOCESE OF BIRMINGHAM BOARD FOR SOCIAL RESPONSIBILITY IN CONJUNCTION WITH SARAH HAYES—SOLICITOR, *Setting Up, Developing and Maintaining a Community Project. A Handbook* (Birmingham, Saros Training Limited, 1998). (Enquiries to the Community Projects and Development Officer, The Diocesan Office, 175 Harborne Park Road, Harborne, Birmingham B17 0BH)

Ann STRICKLEN, Jill McKINNON, SERVE YOUR NEIGHBOUR, WOOLWICH AREA MISSION TEAM, *The Purple Pack for Planning Projects*, 4 Parts, **Part 1—Finding Out** (Southwark Diocesan Board for Church in Society, September 1996); **Part 2—The Planning** Process (Southwark Diocesan Board for Church in Society, September 1996); **Part 3—Setting Up Your Project** (Southwark Diocesan Board for Church in Society, July 1999); **Part 4—Running and Managing Your Project** (work in progress). (Enquiries to Board for Church in Society, Diocese of Southwark, Trinity House, 4 Chapel Court, Borough High Street, London SE1 1HW)

Appendix B: Useful addresses

Advisory, Conciliation and Arbitration Service (ACAS)
Head Office
Brandon House
180 Borough High Street
London SE1 1LW
Tel: 020 7210 3616
Fax: 020 7210 3708
Website: www.acas.org.uk

Scotland
Franborough House
123-157 Bothwell Street
Glasgow G2 7JR
Tel: 0141 204 2677

ACAS Reader Ltd
PO Box 16
Earl Shilton
Leicester LE9 8ZZ
Tel: 01455 852225

ACAS public enquiry points:
Birmingham	Tel: 0121 456 5856
Bristol	Tel: 0117 946 9500
Cardiff	Tel: 029 2076 1126
Fleet	Tel: 01252 811868
Glasgow	Tel: 0141 204 2677
Leeds	Tel: 0113 243 1371
Liverpool	Tel: 0151 427 8881
London	Tel: 020 7396 5100
Manchester	Tel: 0161 833 8585
Newcastle-upon-Tyne	Tel: 0191 261 2191
Nottingham	Tel: 0115 969 3355

Charities Aid Foundation (CAF)
Kingshill
West Malling
Kent ME19 4TA
Tel: 01732 520000
Website: www.charitynet.org

CAF publications are available from:
Biblios
Star Road
Partridge Green
West Sussex RH13 8LD
Tel: 01403 710851

Charity Commission
St Albans House
57-60 Haymarket
London SW1Y 4QX
Tel: 020 7210 4556
Tel: 020 7210 4630 (Fundraising helpline)

Churches' Community Work Alliance (CCWA)
c/o The Revd Brian Ruddock
36 Sandygate
Wath-upon-Dearne
Rotherham S63 7LW
Tel: 01709 873254
Email: ccwa@btinternet.com

Charities Evaluation Services
4 Coldbath Square
London EC1R 5HL
Tel: 020 7713 5722
Fax: 020 7713 5692
Email: enquiries@cesuk1.demon.co.uk

Commission for Racial Equality
Elliot House
10-12 Allington Street
London SW1E 5EH
Tel: 020 7828 7022
Fax: 020 7630 7605
Website: www.cre.gov.uk

Community Development Foundation
60 Highbury Grove
London N5 2AG
Tel: 020 7226 5375
Fax: 020 7704 0313
Email: admin@cdf.org.uk
Website: www.cdf.org.uk

Community Matters
8-9 Upper Street
London N1 0PQ
Tel: 020 7226 0189
Fax: 020 7354 9570
Email: communitymatterslondon@compuserve.com

Croner Publications Ltd
Croner House
London Road
Kingston-upon-Thames
Surrey KT2 6SR
Tel: 020 8547 3333

Department for Education and Employment (DfEE)
Sanctuary Buildings
Great Smith Street
London SW1P 3BT
Tel: 020 7925 5000
Fax: 020 7925 6000
Email: info@dfee.gov.uk
Website: www.dfee.gov.uk

DfEE Publications Centre
PO Box 6927
London E3 3NZ
Tel: 020 7602 2260

DfEE Race Relations Employment Advisory Service
14th Floor, Cumberland House
200 Broad Street
Birmingham B15 1TA
Tel: 0121 244 8141/3

Department of Trade and Industry
1-19 Victoria Street
London SW1E 0ET
Tel: 020 7215 5000
Fax: 020 7222 2629
Website: www.dti.gov.uk

Directory of Social Change
24 Stephenson Way
London NW1 2DP
Tel: 020 7209 5151
Fax: 020 7209 5049

Employment Appeal Tribunal
Audit House
58 Victoria Embankment
London EC4Y 0DS
Tel: 020 7273 1041

Employment Tribunals
Central Office (England and Wales)
19-29 Woburn Place
London WC1H 0LU
Tel: 020 7273 8666

Central Office (Scotland)
Eagle Building
215 Bothwell Street
Glasgow G2 7TS
Tel: 0141 204 0730

Field Support Unit of the Employment Tribunals
100 Southgate Street
Bury St Edmunds IP33 2AQ
Tel: 0345 959775

Equal Opportunities Commission
Overseas House
Quay Street
Manchester M3 3HN
Tel: 0161 833 9244
Fax: 0161 835 1657
Email: info@eoc.org.uk
Website: www.eoc.org.uk

Health and Safety Commission
HSE Information Centre
Broad Lane
Sheffield S3 7HF
Tel: 0114 289 2345
Fax: 0114 289 2333

Health and Safety Executive
Rose Court
2 Southwark Bridge
London SE1 9HS
Tel: 020 7717 6000
Fax: 020 7717 6717

HSE Information Centre
Broad Lane
Sheffield S3 7HQ
Tel: 0541 545500 (helpline)

HSE Publications
PO Box 1999
Sudbury
Suffolk CO10 6FS
Tel: 01787 881165

Regional offices are listed in the telephone directory under Health and Safety Executive.

Inland Revenue
Advice and publications are available from Tax Enquiry Centres and Tax Offices: local contacts listed in the telephone directory under "Inland Revenue". The Inland Revenue also runs a New Employers helpline:
0845 607 0143

Inland Revenue Contributions Agency
For enquiries relating to National Insurance, local contacts are listed in the telephone directory under Inland Revenue Contributions Agency. Advice and leaflets are also available from local social security offices: local contacts listed in the telephone directory under Benefits Agency or Social Security.
Tel: 0345 143143 (helpline)
Information about tax and NICs is on the internet:
Website: www.inlandrevenue.gov.uk

Local Government Management Board
Layden House
76 Turnmill Street
London EC1M 5QU
Tel: 020 7296 6600

London Voluntary Service Council
356 Holloway Road
London N7 6PA
Tel: 020 7700 8107

Manufacturing, Science and Finance union (MSF)
Voluntary Sector Secretary
MSF Centre
33-37 Moreland Street
London EC1V 8BB
Tel: 020 7505 3000
Fax: 020 7505 3030
Website: www.msf.org.uk

The Maternity Alliance
45 Beech Street
London EC2P 2LX
Tel: 020 7588 8582 (Advice and information)

LRD Publications Ltd
78 Blackfriars Road
London SE1 8HF
Tel: 020 7928 3649
Fax: 020 7928 0621
Email: lrd@geo2.poptel.org.uk
Website: www.lrd.org.uk

National Association of Councils for Voluntary Service
3rd Floor, Arundel Court
177 Arundel Street
Sheffield S1 2NU
Tel: 0114 278 6636
Fax: 0114 278 7004

National Council for Voluntary Organisation (NCVO)
Regent's Wharf
8 All Saints Street
London N1 9RL
Tel: 020 7713 6161
Fax: 020 7713 6300
Email: ncvo@ncvo-vol.org.uk
Website: www.ncvo-vol.org.uk

New Ways to Work
309 Upper Street
London N1 2TY
Tel: 020 7226 4026 (helpline)
Tel/Fax: 020 7354 2978
Email: nww@dircon.co.uk

The Pensions Trust
15 Rathbone Street
London W1P 2AJ
Tel: 020 7636 1814

The Stationery Office Books
PO Box 276
London SW8 5DT
Tel: 020 7873 0011 (enquiries)
Tel: 020 7873 9090 (orders)

Trades Union Congress (TUC)
Congress House
Great Russell Street
London WC1B 3LS
Tel: 020 7636 4030
Tel: 020 7467 1294 (publications)
Fax: 020 7636 0632
Website: www.tuc.org.uk

Scottish TUC
333 Woodlands Road
Glasgow G3 6NS
Tel: 0141 337 8100

Transport and General Workers Union
National Secretary for Voluntary Sector Membership
Transport House
16 Palace Street
London SW1E 5JD
Tel: 020 7828 7788
Fax: 020 7963 4440
Email: tgwu@tgwu.org.uk

UNISON
Voluntary Sector
1 Mabledon Place
London WC1H 9AJ
Tel: 020 7388 2366
Fax: 020 7387 6692
Website: www.unison.org.uk